PROTECT YOUR PROFIT

Protect Your Profit

Five Accounting Mistakes and How to Avoid Them

ELIZABETH HALE

COPYRIGHT © 2018 ELIZABETH HALE
All rights reserved.

PROTECT YOUR PROFIT
Five Accounting Mistakes and How to Avoid Them

ISBN   978-1-5445-1298-3   *Paperback*
       978-1-5445-1297-6   *Ebook*

I would like to dedicate this book to my immediate family: Robert, Alexandria, Ryan, and Aspen. You are my inspiration! I really appreciate all of your support. I love you!

CONTENTS

INTRODUCTION 9

PART I: DON'T LET THIS BE YOU
1. BLAMING UNCLE SAM 23
2. DOUBLE-CHECKING THE BOOKS 47
3. MAKING A PROFIT 79
4. STAYING OUT OF DEBT 105
5. BUYING OR SELLING A BUSINESS 123

PART II: GOOD ACCOUNTING PRACTICES
6. MANAGING THE NUMBERS 147
7. RECONCILING YOUR ACCOUNTS 159
8. TAKING INVENTORY 179
9. CUTTING YOUR LOSSES 205
10. BUILDING EQUITY 231
11. GETTING PAID 257
12. BREAKING EVEN 273
13. EMPLOYING FOLKS 297
14. RUNNING THE BUSINESS 319

CONCLUSION 343
ACKNOWLEDGMENTS 353
ABOUT THE AUTHOR 355
APPENDIX 359

INTRODUCTION

Do you think you pay too much in taxes?

Do you worry about an employee embezzling hundreds of thousands of dollars right under your nose?

If you could change one thing in your business that would save you 10% in expenses, thereby adding 10% to your bottom line, would you do it?

Are you struggling with debt?

Do you plan to sell your business or buy a new one?

If you answered yes to any of these questions, this book is for you. If you want to save money and minimize risks of loss, your accounting system is the first place you should look.

HAVE YOU BEEN SWEEPING YOUR ACCOUNTING UNDER THE RUG?

People put off seeking professional accounting help for a variety of reasons.

First, cash is tight at startups. If you've just started your business, professional accounting services probably seem like a luxury. They are not. Accounting is the foundation of any successful business, and you need to make it a priority from day one. I promise you, it will pay off in the long run.

Second, accounting can seem intimidating and complex. Maybe, like many entrepreneurs, you are an idea person and not a numbers person. Maybe you've passed off the accounting to someone else, such as an in-house bookkeeper, and completely forgotten about it. That's what you pay people for, right? Wrong. Even if you have someone else handling the day-to-day accounting tasks, you need to be personally involved. If you do not ask questions and double-check the numbers, you will remain blind to potential red flags.

Even if you are looking at the numbers, are you sure you're looking at the *right* numbers? If you're looking at the wrong numbers, you are bound to draw the wrong conclusions. Too many business owners have a vision of the numbers that simply does not line up with reality. I can't even count the number of times a business owner has assured me they have no issues with receivables, only for me to discover that 50% of their receivables have been sitting unpaid for more than ninety days.

Finally, you may think what you don't know can't hurt you—not true. Deep down, maybe you know that something is amiss, but you're afraid to face reality. Just like taking off your clothes at the doctor's office and putting on a hospital gown, facing your potential money problems can make you feel vulnerable and exposed. Ignoring your problems won't make them go away, though.

If you sweep your accounting under the rug, the numbers will eventually catch up to you, and you will have no choice but to seek professional help. In nearly every case, when clients finally get around to calling me, there is a sense of urgency, because they now have a bigger-picture problem. Often, tens of thousands of dollars and even their business itself is on the line.

WHY CLIENTS COME TO ME

Most of the time, when business owners seek my help, they are feeling frazzled. They don't know if they're making money or not, and they don't understand what's going on when they look at their books.

They've squeaked by for as long as possible without having to dedicate too much money, time, or energy toward accounting, but now they have a major problem. They don't know how to deal with it on their own, so they come to me looking for a plan and structure.

If you're like most of my clients, you are likely seeking accounting help for one of these five primary reasons.

TAXES

Perhaps the IRS or your state tax agency has notified you of a discrepancy, or maybe you're being audited. Or maybe your taxes are higher than expected, and you need help navigating the complex, always-changing tax laws.

EMBEZZLEMENT

Maybe the numbers seem off to you, or maybe you have a bad gut feeling about a team member in charge of the financials. Perhaps you've noticed suspicious transactions or behavior and want an expert's eyes on the matter.

OVERWHELMING DEBT

Perhaps you've passed off the accounting to others, and large amounts of debt have accumulated unnoticed. Now the debts have come due, and you don't have the money to cover them. Or maybe you've been scraping by for months and are tired of never having enough cash.

LOWER-THAN-EXPECTED PROFIT

Maybe you feel like you're making a profit, but you don't have any money to show for your sales and want to know why. Or maybe you're already making a decent profit but want to figure out how to take your returns to the next level.

UPCOMING TRANSACTION OR CHANGE

Last, you may be seeking help proactively. Perhaps you're planning to either buy or sell a business and want to maximize your returns, or maybe you are in the process of scaling your business and want to update your accounting system accordingly.

WHY *YOU* NEED TO THINK ABOUT ACCOUNTING

The number one way to address these five problems is to have a good accounting system in place that you and your employees are disciplined about using. A current, accurate accounting system gives you real-time financial information, providing you the framework within which to make financial decisions.

When you pay attention to your business's accounting

practices, there won't be any surprises. You won't be blindsided by debt or your tax bill, because you will have been tracking your business activity and forecasting for the future. When you understand the weak points of your business and identify potential red flags, you can devise a plan for moving forward.

Besides providing important financial data, your accounting system can also give you information about key performance indicators and nonfinancial metrics, such as the number of sales in a given time, the length of time needed to convert a prospect to a client, and which products or services are most profitable.

You don't need to keep the books yourself, but you do need to have a basic understanding of what is being accounted for and how. If you don't, you cannot successfully manage your team. Without oversight and accountability, you also leave yourself open to embezzlement and poor accounting practices.

Accounting is about more than numbers; it is about the *financial health* of your business. In order to fulfill your vision and meet your goals for the future, you must understand how your business is doing *right now*, on a day-to-day or week-to-week basis.

While you may have others in charge of the day-to-day

accounting tasks, you should be seeing reports on a regular basis. You also must learn to ask the right questions and interpret the numbers so you can verify the information and identify potential red flags. If you're not getting reports and asking questions, there is no way for you to know what's really happening with your business.

You don't need to dedicate a large chunk of time to this task. All it takes is one hour a month spent on focused review of financial performance—just twelve hours a year to check the pulse of your business and make sure everything is OK.

Open your bank statements and look at the bottom line. Flip through the check copies. Scroll through the credit card charges. Do the percentages line up? Have sales increased? What about profit? How much cash does the business currently have in the bank? When you ask your bookkeeper, CPA, or investment adviser questions, do the answers make sense?

As you review key documents and ask questions on a consistent basis, you will begin to identify patterns, and you will be able to zero in on red flags and potential problem areas more quickly. All the time and resources you invest into your accounting now will be well worth it in the long term.

THE RETURN ON INVESTMENT IN ACCOUNTING

A proper accounting system has a huge return on investment (ROI). It saves you money, mitigates risks, and gives you peace of mind. It does all of this by helping you avoid those five common business problems mentioned earlier.

With good accounting, you will save money on taxes. When you know your exact profits and expected taxes, you can implement a variety of strategies to minimize your taxes, such as changing your entity structure or investing in expenses to lower your taxable profit.

An accounting system also provides oversight, thus discouraging embezzlement. If no one is watching and no one is asking any questions, it is easier for employees to steal, and it is easier for those thefts to build up, unnoticed, over a long period. Your accounting system is like your business's security guard. It shows you're not an easy target, and if embezzlement does occur, it will help you identify and put a stop to the theft quickly.

When you dive into the financials of your business, you can identify and prioritize key business issues, which will allow you to avoid overwhelming debt and maximize profit. For example, you can determine which products or services have the highest profit margin so that you can focus attention there. Or you may discover unnecessary spending that can be eliminated, like a monthly subscription for software you no longer use. By constantly increasing your bottom line, you will be better able to continuously scale and grow your business.

Solid accounting also helps in buying or selling a business. Buyers love businesses that have the books in order, and if you plan ahead, you can make strategic financial decisions that will place your business in the most favorable light and get you the best price. If you're buying a business as opposed to selling, being able to identify errors in the business's accounting can mean significant discounts for you.

You can double your money just by investing in a real accounting system for your business. That's right—in 99% of instances, an entrepreneur's ROI in a successful accounting system is 100%. I had one client who had $1.2 million embezzled from her business. The cost of discovering that stolen money was $200,000. So total, her business lost out on $1.4 million. On the surface, dedicating thousands of dollars a month to an accounting system may seem extravagant, but compared to $1.4 million? How could you *not* make that investment? Developing and maintaining a proper accounting system would have cost just a fraction of the loss over the ten years.

Sound accounting practices will give you peace of mind and extra money for business opportunities, and that means direct benefits for you personally.

First and foremost, when you pay attention to your accounting, you will increase your income. The more money your business saves and makes, the more money goes into your pocket. You will also be able to reach your personal and business financial goals faster. The key to achieving goals is developing a solid plan, and that is exactly what a good accounting system helps you do. Whether it is a plan to pay off debt, save x amount of dollars, or make new investments, your accounting system will lay the framework.

By saving you money on taxes and increasing your bottom line, accounting also frees up the cash you need to build and grow your dream business. Cash is king, and having it gives you more options. Few things are as frustrating as having to watch a great opportunity pass by because you don't have the needed cash.

The benefits are clear, but how do you get started?

HOW I CAN HELP

It's easy for me to diagnose accounting issues because I have been doing it for so long. I have worked with small- to medium-size businesses for more than thirty years, and I have seen it all—missed tax incentives worth hundreds of thousands of dollars, long-term embezzlement over many years, and overwhelming debt.

In the first part of this book, I will share real-life examples of these worst-case scenarios to help you build awareness of what you should be looking for and what you should be doing to avoid ending up in a similar situation. (Note that names and details have been changed for privacy.)

In the second part of the book, I will show you how to set up good accounting practices to address or avoid these concerns, and I will teach you how to spot the red flags. I will also detail a few small changes that can have a big impact on your bottom line.

I've spent my career helping businesses make good decisions, and I've been on the other side of the table, too, in your shoes, having owned several businesses and operated a handful more. I believe in the principles of this book because I know they work and because I've seen the consequences of not following them. Trust me, if you want your business to succeed, you *need* a good accounting system.

PART I

Don't Let This Be You

The first part of this book covers the five most common and most disastrous nightmares you might face in your business: paying too much in taxes, suffering employee embezzlement, having lower-than-expected profit, drowning in debt, and getting a bad price when either buying or selling a business. In this section, I will share real-life stories of entrepreneurs and business owners, just like you, who found themselves in these unpleasant situations, and I will briefly touch on how these issues could have been avoided or mitigated with a few simple accounting practices. (The second part of the book will discuss the relevant accounting practices in more detail.)

CHAPTER 1

BLAMING UNCLE SAM

PAYING TOO MUCH TAX—A POTENTIALLY MILLION-DOLLAR MISTAKE

If you think you're paying too much in taxes, you don't even know the half of it. When Steve first came to my accounting firm, eeCPA, for tax help, he thought his taxes were too high, but he had no idea by how much.

For years, Steve did not take proper advantage of the various deductions, credits, and tax strategies available to him (specifically, R&D credits, a deduction for producing goods domestically instead of overseas, and accelerated methods of depreciation of fixed assets). All told, he'd overpaid his taxes by about $1.5 million. That money should have gone to his business. He could have bought new equipment, invested in a new marketing strategy, or given out employee bonuses. Instead, that money went to *taxes*.

Luckily, by amending his past three years of tax returns, we managed to get Steve more than $1 million back in taxes. Unfortunately, you can amend only up to three years of returns. If we'd been able to go back four years—or if Steve had come to us sooner—we could have saved him an additional $500,000. Plus, while he was certainly glad to get all that money back, he still suffered the opportunity cost of not being able to put that money to work for his business sooner.

WHY DO SO MANY PEOPLE PAY TOO MUCH IN TAXES?

Nobody wants to pay more tax than they need to, but for the average person, tax law is a confusing, frustrating maze to navigate. To add further complications, tax law is changing every minute, sometimes quite significantly, as with the many substantial changes that went into effect in 2018.

Staying up to date on the laws requires a commitment of time and energy, and an ability to properly apply changes requires extensive experience. To navigate tax law, you need to know more than just the law; you need to know the interpretation of the law and how the law has been tested in the courts.

You can save tens of thousands of dollars in taxes with the proper knowledge and experience, but that expertise can be difficult to obtain. Even if you hire outside help, you don't always get an expert. Recently, we had a client who had been paying a premium rate to a well-known national firm for his tax filing. When we reviewed his past three years of returns, we discovered many errors, several due to an unfamiliarity with updated laws. Like Steve, this national firm had failed to take advantage of R&D credits as well as the domestic production activities deduction, and they had also miscalculated the alternative minimum tax. There are dozens of different errors you can make when filing your taxes, and if you're not keeping up to date on tax law, it is easy to make expensive mistakes.

Luckily, we will likely be able to get this client $30,000 back in refunds, but his experience is a perfect example of why you need to have a basic understanding of the various tax strategies available to you. To save the most on your taxes, you need expert help, and it is up to you to identify the experts.

If you want to reduce your tax bill and prevent a potentially million-dollar mistake, the first step is to consider your entity structure and your accounting method.

THE MOST IMPORTANT TAX DECISION TO MAKE: ENTITY STRUCTURE

A business's structure has a huge impact on its corresponding taxes. If your business isn't structured properly, you can typically save at least $30,000 in the first three years of business simply by restructuring.

There are four different types of entity structures to consider—C corporations, S corporations, partnerships, and sole proprietorships—and each has pros and cons from a tax perspective.

C CORPORATION

Before the 2018 tax changes, C corporations were taxed as high as 39%. That tax rate has now been reduced to 21%, which sounds great. However, the problem with C corporations is that they are subject to double taxation. Whenever you take money out of a C corporation, such as when distributing earnings to shareholders, that money is taxed again at the shareholder level. So when you take money out of a C corporation, you pay tax twice—21% at the corporate tax rate and then up to 20% at the individual capital gains rate for dividends.

A C corporation is a great choice if you are focusing on building your business. If you intend to reinvest all the business's profits back into the business, then the double taxation does not matter. A C corporation is also typically your best choice if you're doing any R&D work. Unlike other entity structures, C corporations do not have an alternative minimum tax, so if you are doing R&D work, you can take full advantage of the corresponding R&D credits.

Another advantage of C corporations is that they allow you to offer different employee benefit plans, which can be used as part of a tax strategy. Some medical reimbursement plans and owner compensation plans are only available to C corporations.

If you're growing your business in order to sell it, a C corporation is a good structure choice, as selling a C corporation is much easier than an S corporation or sole proprietorship. Plus, when you sell, you can avoid paying tax on gains up to $10 million.

S CORPORATION

If you are living off your company's earnings and constantly taking money out of the business, an S corporation structure would be more beneficial for you than a C corporation.

S corporations are flow-through entities, meaning they are not taxed at the corporate level like C corporations. Rather, the income of the entity is treated as the income of the owners/investors. As a result, S corporations have no double taxation and have a maximum tax rate of 37% (the highest income bracket). As such, depending on your income bracket, you could save a significant amount of money by structuring your business as an S corporation instead of a C corporation.

The major disadvantage of an S corporation is that it is more difficult to sell than a C corporation or partnership and will likely require restructuring to do so.

PARTNERSHIP

If you have a business with partners who have different levels of contribution and different kinds of compensation, a partnership is the way to go.

Partnerships have more flexibility than the other structures. You can have a varying number of partners, and those partners can be treated differently. For example, you could have one money partner and one working partner. The money partner could be guaranteed a percentage of return on his or her capital investment, while the working partner's share is instead based on the business's performance, with no guarantee. Because partnerships, like S corporations, are flow-through entities, different kinds of partners can also pay different amounts of tax, based on the income they receive.

With partnerships, a major tax benefit is that you can put assets in and take assets out without recognizing any kind of gain on the contribution or the distribution of assets or cash. For this reason, real estate investment and development companies almost exclusively use partnerships. Basically, let's say a partnership acquires a piece of property worth $100,000. Over five years, the property appreciates to $125,000. The partnership could then distribute that piece of property to one of the business's partners and would not have to pay any sort of tax on the $25,000 gained in appreciation. If the partner then decided to sell the property, he would have to recognize gain, but the partnership would not.

The final benefit of partnerships is that, like C corporations, they are easier to sell than S corporations or sole proprietorships.

The major disadvantage of partnerships is that for managing members, all of the earnings are subject to a 15.3% self-employment tax (Social Security and Medicare taxes), in addition to normal federal income taxes at up to a 37% rate, plus state taxes.

It is important to note that most partnerships are organized as limited liability companies (for legal reasons), electing to be taxed as partnerships.

SOLE PROPRIETORSHIP

Sole proprietorships are only a good choice if you have a very small business, with less than $50,000 in revenue a year, such as a side business you operate in your spare time.

There are some unique tax advantages to sole proprietorships, though. You can hire your children and pay them a wage and not have to pay FICA taxes on those wages, which saves about 15.3% in self-employment taxes. Similar to C corporations, you can also do health insurance plans with sole proprietorships.

The biggest disadvantage of sole proprietorships is that they have a high audit risk. Nearly one out of ten sole proprietorships are audited, compared to only 0.5% of business returns that are audited.

Additionally, like partnerships, sole proprietorships are subject to self-employment tax in addition to federal income taxes and state taxes.

I recommend that sole proprietorships be organized as single-member limited liability companies. This provides the owner with flexibility for future tax elections and limits the liability (from a legal standpoint).

TAX COMPARISON ACCORDING TO ENTITY STRUCTURE

The following table shows one example of how entity structure can affect the total tax due.

What Form of Business Makes the Most Sense?

Assumptions

Filing Status: Married Filing Jointly
Number of Children: 2
Salary: 100,000
LLC Member Is a Manager: Yes

Specified Service Business: No
Business Income: 250,000
Dividends Reinvested?: No

	Single Member LLC/ Schedule C Sole Proprietorship	Multi-Member LLC/ Partnership	S-Corporation	C-Corp Shareholder
Salary			100,000	100,000
Guaranteed Payment		-		
Dividend Income				142,350
Business Income	249,999	250,000	142,350	
Total Income	249,999	250,000	242,350	242,350
Standard Deduction	(24,000)	(24,000)	(24,000)	(24,000)
Self-Employment Tax Deduction	(11,309)	(11,309)		
Business income deduction	(42,938)	(42,938)	(28,470)	-
Taxable Income	171,752	171,753	189,880	218,350
Child Tax Credit	(4,000)	(4,000)	(4,000)	(4,000)
Self-Employment Taxes	22,617	22,617		
Social Security/ Medicare			7,650	7,650
Income Taxes	29,799	29,800	34,150	29,915
Total Federal Tax	48,416	48,417	37,800	33,565
Net Income after Tax	201,583	201,583	204,550	208,785
		Corporate Tax @ 21%		29,894
		Net to C-Corp Shareholder		178,892

BLAMING UNCLE SAM

HOW YOUR ACCOUNTING METHOD IMPACTS YOUR TAXES
ACCRUAL VERSUS CASH

You can pay tax on either an accrual or a cash accounting method. With the accrual method, you pay tax on any sales that you've booked, even if you haven't received payment yet from your customers. With the cash method, you pay tax only on money you have received.

For financial reporting purposes, you should keep your books on the accrual method so that you can see how your business is actually doing. The cash method takes into account only how much cash you've received and paid out. It doesn't give you any information about pending transactions.

For tax purposes, though, even if you keep your books on the accrual method, you can still file on the cash method with certain parameters. The cash method is often preferred because you only have to pay tax on cash you have actually received. The difference in tax between the accrual and cash method can be significant, frequently $50,000 to $60,000.

Sometimes, though, the accrual method is better. If you're trying to get outside financing, you'll want to use the accrual method so that your financial statements conform with generally accepted accounting principles

(GAAP). You are also required to file under the accrual method if you have a business that has inventory and more than $25 million in average annual gross receipts (sales). (Prior to the Tax Cuts and Jobs Act of 2017, businesses with $10 million or more in average annual sales were required to use the accrual method.)

The accrual method is also useful if you want to take advantage of expensing items without paying for them yet. Cash businesses with low accounts receivable and high accounts payable typically benefit from the accrual method. A restaurant, for example, will have low accounts receivable, because customers pay for their food immediately, but high accounts payable, because they order food and other supplies ahead of time. The restaurant's income will be the same on the cash and accrual methods, because there are no outstanding accounts receivable, but by using the accrual method, the restaurant can claim the unpaid accounts payable as expenses, resulting in a lower taxable profit, which means less tax.

STRAIGHT-LINE DEPRECIATION VERSUS ACCELERATED DEPRECIATION

The depreciation method you choose—straight-line depreciation or accelerated depreciation—has a significant impact on your taxes.

With straight-line depreciation, the asset depreciates the same amount each year. With accelerated depreciation, the asset depreciates more quickly early in its life and then slower later on.

I'm a huge proponent of taking accelerated depreciation. In general, it is always best to write off whatever you can today, because you never know what's coming tomorrow. You never know how or when tax law will change, so it is best to take advantage of deductions when you can.

That said, there are some cases when straight-line depreciation is better. You cannot create a loss with Section 179 depreciation, but you can with the normal method. So if you are in a position where you would like to create a tax loss, you should consider using straight-line depreciation or modified accelerated cost recovery system (MACRS). For the purposes of your books, you want to always use straight-line depreciation. Straight-line depreciation will normalize the expense and increase your net profits, thus the financial performance of your business will look better from a banking/outside-financing perspective.

PRACTICES TO TAX-PROOF YOUR BUSINESS
TIMING OF EXPENSES

One way to tax-proof your business is to time expenses.

If you're using the accrual system for your taxes, you can expense items before paying for them. You will have until March 15 of the following year to pay for the items. For example, you could expense employee paid time off and bonuses in 2018 and wouldn't have to pay them out until 2019. If you're using the cash method, you want to pay and expense everything possible before the year's end to reduce your tax.

You should also time your expenses with regard to future tax changes. At eeCPA, because we anticipated cuts in 2018 with the new tax legislation, we recommended to our clients that they buy as many assets before the end of 2017 as possible. Because their tax rates would be dropping in 2018, it was more important for them to save on taxes in 2017, when rates were still high.

Similarly, if the tax rate is going to increase, as it is scheduled to in 2025, it is best to postpone expenses until the following year, when the tax rate increases and you need the deductions more. It can also be better to take straight-line depreciation instead of accelerated depreciation if you know tax rates are going to increase.

TIMING OF REVENUE

Revenue should be booked only when the product or service is really sold. A salesperson might make a sale, but that sale is not complete until the product or service is delivered/fulfilled.

Even customer deposits aren't technically revenue. You might make a $100,000 sale on December 22 and take a $50,000 deposit from the customer to order the needed materials. If you haven't yet ordered those materials, you aren't recognizing them as an expense, and so you should not recognize the $50,000 as revenue. Otherwise, that money will appear as profit when it's not. If you have to pay 30% tax on that supposed $50,000 profit, then suddenly you're out the $15,000 that you need to purchase materials.

When you're using the cash method, customer deposits can be tricky, because technically, you did receive that cash and thus it should be reported as income. To avoid this issue, you must use explicit language in your contracts stating that customer deposits are not earned or recognized as revenue until a certain milestone has been completed, such as the start of the job or the scheduling of service. If you haven't met the specified terms of the contract and begun the fulfillment work to generate the associated revenue, then the deposit is not really revenue. If your contract instead specifies that customer deposits are nonrefundable earned deposits upon receipt, then they qualify as income, and you must pay taxes on them.

WHEN TO SAVE AND WHEN TO PAY

Everyone wants to save money on taxes, but sometimes it can actually be bad for your business. Saving taxes should be just one part of your overall business strategy, not the exclusive strategy. All good things in moderation!

Amassing a huge amount of debt just to save on taxes is a bad idea. For example, let's say a business owner buys a brand-new Range Rover at $100,000 when a $30,000 Chevy pickup would meet his business's needs. Yes, he might save $30,000 in tax by writing off that Range Rover, but if he doesn't really have the cash to buy the Range Rover, he's committing to debt payments his business may not be able to afford. If he faces a setback—an economic downturn, delayed receivables, a slow month—he will be stuck in a tricky spot, possibly forced to sell off assets at a large discount. His business might even fail, all to save $30,000. Really, though, he's not *saving* $30,000 but spending an additional $70,000. He would have saved much more money by buying the pickup instead and paying slightly more in taxes.

Many people fell into this expensing trap in real estate and construction from 2004 to 2008, making big, unnecessary purchases in order to save on taxes. They were so focused on saving money on taxes that they didn't stop to consider whether they could afford these purchases. Then, when the bubble burst and the recession hit, all their cash was tied up in equipment and real estate. With no liquidity, they found themselves unable to repay their debts and were forced to sell off assets at a huge loss. Some of them lost everything.

You should never spend money just to save on taxes; if you're going to spend money to save on taxes, you should be spending that money on true assets and things your business *needs*.

PRACTICES TO LIMIT AUDIT RISK
GENERAL TIPS

There are dozens of different errors that can trigger an audit—not listing out expenses appropriately, accidentally listing a number as negative instead of positive, listing the cost of sales as exceeding sales, and so on. Because the errors can be incredibly varied, the best way to limit your audit risk is to ensure you have a good set of financial statements and that the numbers make sense.

As mentioned previously, sole proprietorships have a higher audit risk, so simply choosing a different entity structure can also greatly decrease your audit risk.

If anything about your tax return may look suspicious, you can often avoid an audit by preemptively submitting supplemental information to explain why you've done something a certain way.

Finally, be sure to include all information. In the old days, all the relevant tax documents came by mail, clearly marked. Now you may have to log in online to find certain statements, such as your mortgage interest statement.

EMPLOYEES VERSUS INDEPENDENT CONTRACTORS

From a tax perspective, independent contractors are cheaper than employees, as you do not have to pay payroll taxes for independent contractors. Because of this, you may be tempted to save money by classifying employees as independent contractors while still treating them as employees. This shortcut is a major audit risk and is bound to get you in trouble, and the penalties can be severe—up to 50% of the taxes that should have been paid for the misclassified employee.

If you control how a person does the work (e.g., requiring they be at work at certain times), provide them all the tools to do the job, or give them benefits, that person is truly an employee and not an independent contractor, no matter how you classify them.

If you are paying someone $5,000 a month, you can save

about 15% in payroll taxes, or $750 a month, by classifying that person as an independent contractor instead of an employee. Now, let's say that person goes to claim unemployment, even though they know they were an independent contractor. All of a sudden, you're being audited. If the government determines that the person was truly an employee and not an independent contractor, you will have to pay all the back taxes that should have been paid as well as the penalty. Because you wanted to save $750 a month, you now have to pay $1,125 ($750 in owed taxes plus $375 in penalty) per month of misclassification. Because the misclassification is sometimes not discovered for two to three years, the cost of this unexpected bill can be astronomical—$27,000 to $40,500 in this example.

Besides the potential tax penalties, misclassification of employees also opens you up to legal liabilities. If a supposed independent contractor gets hurt while working for you and you don't have the appropriate workers' compensation policy, you will be in deep trouble.

You also won't be able to sell your business, because buyers won't want to be responsible for the tax penalties of the misclassification, which is likely to be discovered in due diligence.

Independent contractors are often not good for a business overall, as you do not have much control over these individuals. They can leave and go work for someone else at any point, and noncompete agreements for independent contractors can be incredibly difficult to enforce, if you can get them to agree to such agreements at all. If you're dead set on having independent contractors, though, you should contract only with companies—that is, you should contract with an independent contractor's LLC, as opposed to the individual. In this way, you can avoid many of the risks of that person being considered an employee instead of an independent contractor.

PRACTICES TO SHELTER PROFIT FROM TAX

It takes money to make money, and in this case, it takes money to save money, too. There are a variety of different deductions and strategies you can take advantage of to shelter profit from tax, but many of them require money.

You can give out employee bonuses or offer employee benefit plans, such as tax-sheltered retirement plans. You can make charitable donations, including land or conservation donations (often, you can buy land at a deeply discounted rate but then claim it for a greater amount [the fair market value] when you donate it, effectively lowering your tax rate by anywhere from 30% to 50%). You can set up a captive insurance company (a type of self-insurance).

Other methods don't require as much cash investment but do require planning and strategy. If you employ your children, you can take certain deductions. You can count home office expenses. You can take auto deductions, using either the standard mileage rate or the actual expenses incurred, whichever is higher. If you sell intangibles such as software abroad and domestically, you can set up a separate corporation to handle all your foreign sales so that you can get an additional 37.5% deduction, thus effectively reducing the 21% standard corporate rate to 13.125%, as well as providing other tax benefits. We just did this at eeCPA for a software company, and this single change is saving them about 8% in tax. They just signed a new $5 million contract for software in Australia, so they're going to save about $400,000 right off the bat.

There are dozens upon dozens of different strategies you can use to save money on taxes, but it is important to customize the strategies to your specific needs, based on your current business concerns and your plan and vision for the future. Tax strategy is not black and white, and what works for someone else, even someone in the same industry as you, may not be the best solution for your business.

The best way to maximize your tax savings is to consult a professional, who will analyze your specific business needs and circumstances and craft the best plan accordingly.

WHAT IF YOU ARE ALREADY IN OVER YOUR HEAD?

If you're already stuck with a large tax debt, you should make good on the debt and move forward. Although it may be tempting, you should avoid looking backward and trying to do a ton of historical work. Your top priorities should be cleaning up the issues in the current period, developing a plan to pay the debt, and tweaking your system so you don't face the same problems again. Only once you get your house in order should you look into amending past returns.

If you have a large tax bill, you don't need to pay it in one lump sum. The government is willing to offer installment agreements that will spread your tax bill out over a longer period. Also, if you are unable to pay your taxes because your financial circumstances have changed, whether due to a death, divorce, a failed business, or anything else, you can take advantage of an *offer in compromise* in which the government agrees to accept a small portion of your total debt as complete payment.

If you think the amount you owe is inaccurate or if you're facing an audit with a lot of money on the line, you should seek professional help. In the case of an audit, you'll want to look for a CPA, tax attorney, or enrolled agent, as they are the only ones who can represent a taxpayer before the IRS. If, for example, you used a Certified Financial Planner to prepare your taxes, you will need to hire someone else to represent you in the audit.

That's what happened to Amelia. She had a Certified Financial Planner prepare her tax returns, but then she was audited, and her financial planner couldn't represent her. So she came to eeCPA.

In this audit, she was facing potentially $250,000 in owed taxes. The main issue: the IRS was denying a number of the business's claimed deductions. The business had a lot of meals, entertainment, marketing, and promotion deductions, which are common target areas for the IRS.

Right away, we set to work cleaning up the financial records for the audited period. Luckily, we were able to re-create promissory notes and find all the supporting material needed to justify the deductions. If Amelia had a reliable accounting system in place, then all of this material would have already been readily available, and she wouldn't have needed to spend so much time and money correcting the issue retroactively. In any case, we amended the returns, which had been prepared incorrectly and had actually *omitted* some valid deductions, and managed to get Amelia off the hook for the $250,000 in taxes. At the end of the day, Amelia saved a hefty chunk of change and learned a valuable lesson in the process.

KEY TIPS

- **Have a good accounting system.** This is a must. Your tax strategy will depend heavily on your business's financial data, so this information must be accurate. Without knowing the facts of your business, it is nearly impossible to develop a strategy in alignment with your specific circumstances and vision for your business.
- **Have cash available to fund your tax-saving plan.** You might be able to save $5,000 by purchasing $20,000 of needed equipment, but if you don't have $20,000 to spend, it doesn't matter. Without cash reserves, you don't have nearly as many tax-saving options.
- **Start thinking about taxes early.** If the year is already over, you still have some options you can take advantage of up until April 15, but they're limited. Most things need to be done much earlier than December. For example, if you want to save taxes by creating a retirement plan, you typically need it up and running by September 30. Remember, this is a tax strategy, a *plan*. It must be forward-thinking, not a last-minute scramble. At eeCPA, we can find ways to hustle and save clients money even after certain deadlines have passed, but your savings will be much more significant if you are proactive with your strategies.
- **Keep your accounting system up to date.** Because

the timing of your tax strategy is so important, it is critical that your accounting system is up to date. You have to know exactly where your profits stand, and you have to track and time your receivables and expenses.

FURTHER INFORMATION

- To learn more about entity structures, including how to choose the proper structure for your business, see chapter 10, "Building Equity."

CHAPTER 2

DOUBLE-CHECKING THE BOOKS

EMBEZZLEMENT—JUST A "LITTLE" OFF THE TOP

Before becoming an eeCPA client, Marianne hired a bookkeeper to take care of her financials. This bookkeeper, Jody, quickly noticed something. Marianne never opened her bank statements, never looked at canceled checks or check copies, and never asked questions. This presented Jody with an opportunity she thought was too good to pass up: within ninety days of being hired, she began embezzling.

Marianne owned one of the most highly regarded sign companies in the area. She'd first started her business back in the late eighties, making custom name badges for nurses at eighty-five cents a pop, including delivery. She delivered a quality product on time and even provided customization according to her clients' needs. As a result, her company quickly grew. She was soon doing $10 million-plus in business annually and had very lucrative contracts with a number of big-name *Fortune* 100 companies. With this level of success, her business was obviously generating a lot of cash, so she didn't notice when some started to go missing—just a little bit skimmed off the top, courtesy of Jody.

In fact, Marianne didn't notice anything was wrong for *ten years*, and the embezzlement could have gone on for another ten years or more if not for one man—James. James was a tenant in a building Marianne owned, and he actually had his own sign business, in the niche market of new housing developments. With the 2008 housing crash, new housing developments ceased being built. His business took a corresponding blow, and he fell behind on his rent.

Marianne noticed James wasn't paying his rent and wanted to help him out. She let him out of his lease and also hired him to help drive efficiency and productivity at her company because he had skills that were complementary to what her business needed.

James was a very analytical person, and part of his familiarization with her company included reviewing the accounting system to see where it could be improved. In the course of his review, he was surprised to find himself as a payee of several checks in the ledger. He'd just filed bankruptcy for his failed business, and he knew that he hadn't received that money. Clearly, something was wrong with the books. His findings sparked further investigation that uncovered Jody's massive embezzlement scheme.

For ten years, Jody had been stealing money right under Marianne's nose. Marianne trusted Jody implicitly and wasn't paying attention, making it easy for Jody to embezzle. She simply wrote checks to herself and to her own personal American Express bill but then recorded these checks in the accounting system as if they were written to the business's common vendors.

Once this embezzlement was uncovered, the attorney general got involved, and Jody is now serving jail time and has a judgment against her for the amount of money that was stolen. But Jody stole so much that the chances of Marianne ever seeing that full amount of money again are slim to none.

So exactly how much did Jody manage to steal? *$1.2 million*. A "little off the top" can add up pretty quickly when the embezzlement goes unnoticed for years. On average, Jody stole about $100,000 every year, just 1% of the business's total revenue. Because the business was bringing in so much money, Marianne didn't notice the loss. However, if she'd simply been reviewing the check copies, she would have noticed the embezzlement right away. And if Jody knew Marianne was double-checking, she likely wouldn't have tried to steal in the first place.

WHY DOES EMBEZZLEMENT HAPPEN SO FREQUENTLY?

If you think your business isn't at risk for embezzlement, think again. Plenty of smart people have fallen victim to fraud and embezzlement precisely because they don't think they're at risk.

Many people wrongly assume that small businesses have a lower risk for embezzlement. The 2016 Hiscox embezzlement study found that four of every five victim organizations had fewer than one hundred employees and just under half had fewer than twenty-five employees.[1]

Embezzlement is a huge issue—the Hiscox study calculated the average loss as $807,443[2]—but it often goes unnoticed because the business owner is blinded by their

---

1 Hiscox, *The 2016 Hiscox Embezzlement Study*, https://www.hiscox.com/documents/14537-US-2016-Hiscox-Embezzlement-Study.pdf.

2 Ibid.

relationship with the embezzler. Marianne had a fantastic relationship with Jody. They were very close, and Marianne thought Jody had her back. As a result, Marianne overlooked a lot of things and trusted Jody to do her job and handle all the financials. Trust is a big issue—you can't trust blindly.

Many business owners hear only what they want to hear and see only what they want to see, and of course you don't *want* to discover that one of your trusted employees is stealing from you. But you are running a business. It is your job to make sure your employees are doing their jobs correctly, and that means you need to double-check your books; you can't just take your employees' word that everything is OK. If you're not paying attention and double-checking, it's like you're leaving your house unlocked with a big sign on the front lawn saying you're not home. In other words, you are leaving yourself open to be robbed.

There are a few different reasons you might not be double-checking your business's financials. Sometimes it comes down to intimidation. You may be intimidated by a certain person or by the financial complexities in general. The person in charge of your financials might seem completely in control of the situation. They may say intelligent things and take ownership of the work, and they may get defensive or even aggressive if you question that work. They may explain things in a purposely complex or confusing way in order to intimidate you with all the intricacies of the financials.

As a result of the aggression and confusing nature of the financials, you may decide that they do have it under control and stop questioning them. Then, before you know it, you're in a position of being completely reliant on this person. They become 100% responsible for all the financials, and no one is policing them but themselves.

You also might not be double-checking because you have bigger fish to fry. On any given day, you probably have a dozen different things demanding your attention. Many business owners think it is beneath them to be looking at bank and credit card statements when they have other, "more important" things to focus on.

But you double-check when you lock your car, right? You give a test pull of the handle, or you press the lock button and listen for the beep. You need to put the same care into your business. Embezzlement happens when there are no checks and balances, no accountability. Even if you have a CPA or a CFO, you need to verify that person's work.

The good news is that it takes only one hour a month. Set aside that time to review financial source documents, such as check copies and bank statements, and to check in with your key clients and vendors. This is all part of staying on top of your business.

THE RED FLAGS OF EMBEZZLEMENT AND FRAUD

When searching for warning signs of embezzlement, focus your attention on people in management roles and people in finance/accounting positions, as those with the most access to and control over the money have the greatest opportunity to embezzle. The Hiscox embezzlement study found that more than 40% of thefts were committed by an employee in a finance/accounting function, and in the majority of cases, managers were more likely than employees to steal.[3]

The first red flag that an employee may be untrustworthy is resistance to inquiries. If the person in charge of your financials gets defensive or aggressive when you ask for documents, you have a problem.

You also have a problem if that person delays giving you reports that should be immediately available. It's a sign that they need to cook the books before handing information over to you. They might give excuses that sound reasonable, such as, "I'm so busy right now working on this other project you gave me last week, but I'll get to it." You can give your employees the benefit of the doubt

---
[3] Ibid.

the first couple of times, but if it becomes a pattern, look into it.

Also, if your bookkeeper has a new priority every week, your alarm bells should start going off. Even if that employee isn't actively embezzling, there is a strong chance they're overwhelmed and may be letting things slip through the cracks accidentally.

Trust your gut. If you have a bad feeling about an employee and think embezzlement may be happening, investigate. The first things you should look at are bank accounts and credit cards, check fraud, and payroll. Even if you don't think embezzlement is occurring, you should be keeping an eye on these areas as well as watching out for potential cases of "unintentional" fraud.

AT-RISK AREAS FOR FRAUD
BANK ACCOUNTS AND CREDIT CARDS

If any of your employees have access to company bank accounts or credit cards, they have a chance to commit fraud.

One common type of fraud in this area is using company funds on unqualified purchases. For example, one of my clients had an employee who was using the company debit card to fill up not only her personal gas tank but also her entire family's gas tanks.

With access to company bank accounts, employees can even redirect funds directly to their personal accounts. This happened in a case of embezzlement I dealt with at a doctors' office. The business was doing well, and the doctors were receiving more money than they ever had before, so they thought everything with the business was on track. But in reality, the financial controller had increased the business's line of credit. The doctors were only getting more money each month because of this increase in credit, which the doctors would eventually be held liable for. Meanwhile, the controller had control of the bank accounts and was diverting business funds to a personal account via phony vendor payments. He was also diverting money by buying different gift cards and claiming to give them to other employees while using them himself.

Bank accounts and credit cards are key areas for embezzlement, so you need to carefully and systematically review all statements. If you aren't reviewing the statements, you won't notice any suspicious transactions.

CHECK FRAUD

Check fraud is what happened with Marianne. The controller at the doctors' office also committed check fraud. He would bury checks in a stack of papers for the doctors to sign, not attached to invoices or bills, and the doctors would blindly sign the checks without looking at the payees or the amounts. He committed further check fraud in a fairly clever way: he got personal credit cards at the same institutions the doctors had, so they signed checks to pay off his credit card bills while thinking they were paying off their own bills.

I've also seen instances of embezzlement in which a check that was made out to a business, such as a payment from an insurance company, was posted in the billing system but then the money never made it into the business's bank account, as the person in charge of cashing it took the money for themselves instead. If someone has check-signing authority, a signature stamp, or some basic forgery skills, they can sign the back of a check for the business and then make it payable to themselves and cash it out. Much of the time, the bank won't catch this, especially if the individual chooses to deposit the check at an ATM.

PAYROLL

The payroll system is also commonly at risk for fraud. Employees might take advances on their paychecks and never pay those advances back, or worked hours could be falsified or pay rates adjusted. Sometimes you might even have false employees on the payroll, receiving a wage despite not existing. Those false wages are then directly deposited into the embezzler's account.

The solution is simple: review the payroll records and reports, and determine who is getting paid. If you see scheduled hours that don't make sense, an unusually high pay rate, or a name you don't recognize, then—ding, ding, ding—you found an issue.

You also want to make sure you have appropriate onboarding and offboarding processes for employees to limit potential mistakes, as sometimes payroll issues are oversights and not intentional. In these cases, the fraud falls under the next category of "unintentional" fraud, where the fraud is not a result of malicious intent.

"UNINTENTIONAL" FRAUD

It's not always the case that somebody is trying to intentionally steal from you. While cases of conscious embezzlement are usually the most tragic and devastating, especially because of the human factor—the feeling of betrayal and the loss of trust—they account for only a fraction of instances of fraud.

I had one client who was booking a bunch of sales but then found himself unable to collect on the receivables. The issue, it turned out, was that the salespeople were compensated based on when they made a sale, not based on when the customer paid. As a result, the salespeople would book sales but tell the customers they could pay later. In many cases, the salespeople would end up being paid commission for a sale that was later canceled.

Make sure you link sales incentives to customer payment and fulfillment of the sale instead of the booking of a sale. Even if the customer pays a deposit for work that isn't scheduled for, say, another six months, you need to be wary of paying out commissions. If that deposit is refundable, the customer can cancel and get their money back, and you will have paid out a commission on a contract that never actually took place. While you may not feasibly be able to hold on to the salesperson's commission payment for six months, you at least need to have a system in place to track canceled sales in order to ensure commissions can be adjusted appropriately.

Another common type of fraud is postponing the recording of expenses. Expenses should be recorded the date they're incurred or committed to, but some people will get vendors to issue postdated bills so that they can get the supplies they need while making it look like they didn't spend that money. Doing this makes it look like they're within their budget when they're really not.

Finally, another common type of fraud occurs when employees simply fall behind on their work. You might have a part-time bookkeeper who is completely overwhelmed but doesn't want to say anything for fear of risking their job. Bills could be piling up in a drawer, not entered into the system, resulting in a financial picture of your business that is completely inaccurate.

FIRST STEPS TO PREVENTING FRAUD
MAKING GOOD HIRES

You absolutely must be diligent about background checks when hiring people to be in charge of your financials. Most people who commit fraud are repeat offenders. If one of your employees is going to embezzle from your company, they've likely done so before, probably in other states, so you need to do a thorough background check for any kind of criminal activity. Search anywhere the person has lived in the last ten years. Because these people will often move states, you should do a national criminal search in addition to a local one.

Check potential hires' credit reports as well as criminal records. Credit reports tell a lot about a person's character. Do they pay back their debts? Do they pay people on time? Do they take ownership of the debts they incur, or do they commit to things they know they can't afford?

These tests can cost anywhere from $100 to $200 per hire, but having this information is invaluable. Oftentimes, you will discover other things from a background check besides potential to commit fraud. For example, you might discover a potential hire has been arrested for domestic violence. The info you gain will indicate what kind of person the new hire will be in your workplace. If you don't gather the data and at least have a discussion with the potential new hire about any questionable information, you could be letting the fox into the henhouse unguarded.

In addition to running background checks, be sure to assess the skill level of potential new hires and follow up with references to verify their alleged qualifications. Everyone thinks bookkeeping is easy, and many people hold themselves out as bookkeepers when they're really not qualified. If your bookkeeper isn't organized and trained properly, then maybe they'll be able to keep track of receipts, but they won't be able to properly manage your accounting system.

When we take on a new client at eeCPA, we often find that they have no comprehensive system for the financials. They may use one system for invoicing, another for making expenditures, and then they just randomly write checks or give credit cards out. With a system like that, no bookkeeper is set up for success, especially one with little to no formal training, as is often the case.

When you're hiring a bookkeeper, you need to find someone who is organized, methodical, and consistent in their approach to accounting. And if you don't have a good system already in place, you need to hire someone who has previous experience building a system from scratch.

I've found that instead of hiring such a person, most businesses end up in one of the following two scenarios.

First, the bookkeeper is the business owner's significant other, who has little to no real-world experience or training. If your bookkeeper doesn't have the proper experience, then mistakes *will* be made. They won't enter transactions into the ledger properly, and then the numbers you're working from will be inaccurate.

Or second, the bookkeeper is a young woman who has been hired to run the office in general. She has to keep the books, answer phone calls, maybe even sell things on the phone. With so many different tasks on her plate, she can get sidetracked easily, resulting in errors or a backlog of work. Just like in the first scenario, when reports are pulled, they're not realistic, which will make it difficult to make effective business decisions and spot potential fraud.

Hiring someone at $10 or $15 an hour to manage all these moving parts without any formal training or an accounting system in place is unlikely to be successful for your business in the long run. Generally speaking, someone who is appropriately trained, has the proper education, and is familiar with the system and the business operation itself is not going to be available for hire at or near minimum wage.

When you're running a startup and money is tight, sometimes you're forced into cutting corners, but I've seen these same issues at businesses doing more than $2 million a year in revenue. As your business grows, once you have the funds, you need to invest in your accounting personnel, as investing in a system with the right people and the right processes is the first step to preventing fraud.

THE EECPA SYSTEM

At eeCPA, we set up an entire system based on the individual client's needs. We take every original record, such as invoices, estimates given to customers, and expenditure receipts, and we attach it directly to the relevant transaction in the accounting system. So if you pull up a particular transaction, you will have the corresponding paper trail right there.

Then we set up a whole process, detailing all the needed steps and their order, and we put it all in the cloud. This way, the client can log in from any device and see everything with total transparency: What steps on this project have been completed? What does my team need to do?

What was this check for? Where is this bill? What documentation, if any, is missing? We tie the entire system back to the sale, so absolutely every single step and cost associated with the sale is accounted for. Whether it's the cost of your own employees providing a service or the cost of having to purchase needed materials, everything is recorded.

Sometimes we have to integrate other systems, such as outside billing or sales-tracking systems. For healthcare, for example, many doctors' offices will record received patient and insurance payments in their accounting system while keeping all their billing in another system. If the accounts aren't reconciled each month, unpaid accounts can easily slip through the cracks, along with other mistakes, such as the use of the wrong insurance codes, resulting in not being paid. If the billing data isn't imported into the accounting system, it is nearly impossible to spot the trends and red flags that would alert you to an issue. As a result, maybe you don't discover that you used the wrong insurance codes for three months. Then you have to resubmit three months' worth of billing and then wait another sixty to ninety days to get paid. Such severe disruptions to your cash flow can put a tremendous strain on your business.

To prevent such mistakes, it is important to pull all the relevant data from any outside systems directly into the accounting system.

THREE BASIC STEPS TO PREVENTING EMBEZZLEMENT

There are three basic procedures you need to follow to protect your business from fraud and embezzlement.

1. Have a system in place.

If you're not tracking the data, then of course you won't notice any inconsistencies or issues.

2. Keep up to date with the system.

Your system is only as good as the information in it. You can't have a system where people work on it only now and then, whenever they get a chance. You have to pay your vendors on a regular schedule, and your invoices have to go out to your customers on a regular schedule if you want to get paid on a regular schedule. People tend to let things slip or slide here and there, but you need to have a set, consistent schedule to ensure that the data you're working from is accurate and up to date. Have scheduled dates to pay your vendors and your employees. Close your books on a certain date each month and make sure all the invoices and bills are entered into the system daily or weekly. And put an alert in place to notify you if anything deviates from the schedule so that you can get caught up as soon as possible.

3. Have an approval process.

Ideally, you should have an approval process and checklist that has been designed for your specific business to double-check payments going out, review source documents (e.g., bank statements and canceled checks), and review payroll. You shouldn't have to manage the day-to-day specifics, but you should be getting regular reports, daily and weekly, as part of the approval process.

THE IMPORTANCE OF DOUBLE-CHECKING

I can't stress enough how important it is to double-check, no matter how much you trust the person in charge of your financials. I even want my clients to double-check *my* work. I already double- and triple-check my own work, so I know there aren't likely to be mistakes, and I know that I'm not embezzling, but I want double-checking to become second nature for my clients. It is that important.

It's not just individuals you need to double-check either. You can't always trust other companies to do their jobs appropriately, as I discovered for one of my eeCPA clients.

This client owned a telemarketing company that processed about $2.4 million a year in credit card transactions. Because the company was doing phone sales, the transactions were high risk and resulted in a lot of chargebacks after people changed their minds about their purchases. The company didn't have anyone comparing what was sold to what money actually got to their bank account, so they hired eeCPA to evaluate and compare their merchant credit card statements against their bank accounts.

They were using a merchant processor to process the transactions, and we ended up finding a shortfall of approximately $500,000 over a three-year period. For this period, the merchant processor was producing statements showing the $500,000, but those funds were never deposited into the client's bank account.

The merchant processor industry can be quite corrupt, as it is fairly unregulated and there are a lot of layers involved where things can fall through the cracks. One of the big issues we found in this instance had to do with the reserve account.

Depending on your industry, the merchant processor may withhold a certain amount from your sales, such as 10%, to cover potential chargebacks. This 10% is in addition to their 3% fee (plus other fees that aren't always fully disclosed in the beginning). The merchant processor holds on to the reserve funds and determines when they will give that money back to you. They're supposed to release the reserve over time, but a lot of them don't. So if you make $10,000 in sales one month, the merchant processor will take around $300 for fees plus an additional $1,000 in reserve, taking $1,300 total out of that $10,000.

In the case of my telemarketing client, the merchant processor was making adjustments to the reserve, reducing it by hundreds of thousands of dollars for no reason. Anytime you see an adjustment on a statement from a vendor, you should investigate. In this case, some of the reduction was valid—funds used to cover chargebacks. But the vast majority of the money just disappeared, with no accounting for it. In my opinion, this was not a mistake but deliberate fraud.

Merchant processors don't give you statements about what is in your reserve account, so it is up to you to keep track of what your sales are, what money is being held in reserve, what money is being removed for fees, and what your chargebacks are. Otherwise, it is easy for merchant processors to take advantage of you.

The telemarketing company has a lawsuit against the merchant processor pending right now, but in many ways, it is too late. Unfortunately, this telemarketing company has gone out of business, as they did not have enough cash to make ends meet. If they'd had that $500,000 income they were supposed to have, maybe things would have turned out differently.

PRACTICES TO FRAUD-PROOF YOUR BUSINESS

When it comes to fraud and embezzlement, current assets and liabilities are the issue. For assets, you want to look at things such as your business's cash, received checks, and inventory. For liabilities, you want to look at things such as outgoing checks, credit cards, outstanding invoices, and lines of credit.

In all these areas, there are some pretty simple strategies you can implement to reduce your risk. These strategies don't require a lot of thought and are mostly common sense, but they're the kinds of things that often fall by the wayside when you're busy and focused on growing your business. Remembering to do these tiny things can make a huge difference. In all cases, having simple, transparent systems is critical.

CASH PRACTICES

Cash includes the physical cash at a store location (including received checks), petty cash, and gift cards. Proper cash practices are absolutely critical to preventing fraud. For example, one of my clients didn't have a system in place to do a physical count of the cash on hand at the business, relying only on the report of what cash they should have. The employees knew no one came by to actually count the cash, so they began giving themselves payroll advances in cash while saying that the cash was still in the store when it really wasn't.

Follow these procedures for physical cash:

- Have good deposit practices. If your business is cash-heavy, institute daily deposits.
- Make sure deposits are verified by the bank.
- Have a check-scanning machine in your office so that funds can be deposited without having to go to the bank.
- Physically count the cash and make sure it balances out.

Follow these procedures for petty cash:

- Keep a log of how much petty cash is used and on what.
- Retain all receipts for purchases made with petty cash. You could choose to implement a reimbursement system, where employees must first present a receipt to get the petty cash.
- Set limits on how much petty cash employees can use for various expenses and require approval for purchases over that amount.
- Establish checks and balances for petty cash distribution. Have one person doling out the petty cash and collecting receipts, and another person spending the petty cash.

Follow these procedures for gift cards:

- Have a gift card log that documents the number of gift cards purchased and the dollar amount of the gift cards. If you buy a hundred $25 Starbucks gift cards, that's $2,500. That's not exactly chump change, so that money should definitely be logged.
- Hold gift cards in a secured, locked area. You want to treat them exactly as if they were physical cash.
- Have an approval process for gift cards that a manager has to sign off on. Don't just hand gift cards out.
- Document who receives the gift cards and why.

CHECK PRACTICES

Follow these procedures for writing and signing checks:

- Don't use a signature stamp. If you use a signature stamp, all someone has to do is "borrow" it, and then they can start making checks out left and right.
- Require approvals for all bill payments, and don't give anyone check-signing authority without rules and limitations. Limit the number of check signers to just one or two people.
- Never sign a check that isn't directly attached to a bill.
- Sign checks in one batch so that you don't lose track of what you're signing. If you're signing one check every day, it is a lot easier to not realize that you might

be signing two checks in the same week for the same vendor.
- Review check copies. Now, with so much of banking happening online, you may have to specifically request and pay a small fee (e.g., $3 a month) so that check copies will be delivered to you on your monthly statement.
- In general, try to limit the number of checks that you write and do more electronic transactions instead, such as direct ACH. A lot of banking systems will allow you to set up an approval process for electronic transactions, so if somebody submits a payment invoice, then someone in management has to approve it before the payment is issued to the vendor.

CREDIT CARD PRACTICES

Anytime you give an employee a company credit card, you must establish clear rules and limitations. I recommend following these best practices:

- Always use credit cards over debit cards. With a debit card, someone has direct access to your bank account. By the time you realize there's fraud, the money is already gone. Banks will reimburse fraudulent charges, but it takes time—time when you might need that money and don't have it. Plus, once your debit card is compromised, you may have to close your account and open a new one, which is a hassle. With fraudulent charges on a credit card, you don't have to worry about being reimbursed. You just have to dispute the charge so you don't have to pay for it, and then you have to get a new credit card. As an added bonus, credit cards come with points and reward systems that essentially give you free money.

- Determine what kind of expenses employees may use the card for and how much they are allowed to spend each day. For example, on business trips, establish a per diem allowance for food.
- Establish a dollar amount at which employees need to get approval from a superior for a transaction.
- Set credit card limits for each cardholder. You can set single-purchase, daily, and monthly limits, as long as you open an appropriate business credit card account. You can also set different limits for different people. Maybe your lower-level team can charge up to $500 for x purchases, and then for anything over $500, they need to get management approval. Maybe your middle-management team can make purchases without approval up to $1,000.
- Analyze the average spending patterns per person, either by reviewing receipts or credit card/bank statements. Once you determine the average spending patterns, investigate anything out of the norm. For example, if you notice four gas receipts per day for one person, you will immediately know something fishy is going on.

PROCESSES TO REVIEW AND DOUBLE-CHECK YOUR FINANCIAL INFORMATION

As mentioned previously, your accounting system is only as good as the information in it, so you want to double-check that the information in your system is accurate. For example, often bills won't be properly entered into the system, making it look like the business is more profitable than it really is, because all the expenses haven't been factored in. There could be a whole pile of payables sitting in someone's drawer, not entered into the system, and you might not find out until some vendor calls to ask why they haven't received payment yet.

Follow these procedures to double-check the information in your accounting system:

- Call your top ten vendors and make sure there are no outstanding invoices.
- Compare your customers' contracts with the invoices they received, as the two might be different.
- Attach all the original records to the relevant transactions. With today's technology, you can attach a customer contract directly to the receivables transaction or add an invoice from a vendor directly to a payables transaction to get full transparency.
- Do an independent spot check of inventory, with a separation of duties between at least two people. Have one person who is in charge of purchasing the

inventory and tracking what is supposed to be there, and have another person physically count the inventory and verify it's there. (Practices for tracking and counting inventory are discussed in further detail in chapter 8, "Taking Inventory.")
- Review source documents. Scan through bank account statements, review credit card accounts and charges per person, and keep copies of canceled checks on hand.
- Ask questions! Ask your bookkeeper or whoever is in charge of the financials questions about the information they're giving you: Has every single bill been posted here? Has every single invoice been recorded? Does this report include the most recent expenditures? Have all the banking and credit card transactions been posted? Have these accounts been reconciled?

COST OF GOODS, SALES, AND REVENUE

There was a pizzeria in New York that was underreporting its income, which is pretty common in cash-intensive businesses such as pizzerias, but how the IRS figured this out was pretty genius.

The IRS knew that it takes so many cups of flour to make dough for one pizza, and they knew how much flour the pizzeria had purchased. Based on interviews with the owners and the management team of the pizzeria, the IRS also knew that the pizzeria wasted very little food, barely throwing out more than one pizza's worth of dough each night.

So with the data for how many cups of flour were required per pizza, how much flour was purchased, and how much flour was thrown out, the IRS determined the pizzeria was selling $25,000 of pizza a month. The pizzeria was reporting sales of only $10,000 a month, though. Busted.

What business owners often don't realize is that a lot of times when you're auditing a set of books, you're not just looking at the sales—you're also looking at the costs. If you spend x amount on costs, you expect to make y amount in profit. By looking at your costs, you can determine what your sales should have been and pick up on potential discrepancies in the books.

The first step is to establish a baseline of data so that you know what that cost-to-sales ratio is. Once you have the baseline, you have a clear way to measure your business results. If you don't make the amount of revenue you would expect based on costs, you can start investigating what happened to cause the discrepancy.

When you're looking at costs and corresponding revenue, you don't want to look at just money and transactions.

You also want to talk to your team about what's happening. Ask questions such as, "Was there any tossed product? Was any of the product damaged?"

In the cannabis industry, for example, based on how many seeds were planted, how many plants can fit in a room, how many lights are in a room, and other factors, you can determine how many pounds of cannabis you should yield. If that amount isn't produced, embezzlement could be the cause, but there are other explanations too. So start making inquiries. What happened to the difference? Was it stolen? Was it tossed? Why? Did it dry out? Get stale? Were the plants not taken care of? Did they get moldy? Did someone screw up and not have the lights on? Was the air quality bad?

Sometimes you will find honest errors that can be corrected to increase your profit, and sometimes you will find that there aren't any reasonable answers for the discrepancy, tipping you off to potential fraud.

WHAT IF FRAUD HAS ALREADY HAPPENED?

If fraud has already happened, you should fire your CPA and hire a new one. In fact, hire a whole new finance team. Now is the time to bring in expert help.

You should then do a thorough audit of all your books.

Once you know fraud has occurred, you need to determine the extent of the fraud.

Then set up good accounting practices—better late than never. If fraud has happened once, it could happen again, so take measures to prevent that from happening.

Finally, start legal action. In a lot of cases, you won't be able to recoup all the money lost, but you won't get anything back if you don't start legal action.

KEY TIPS

- **Be diligent and disciplined in reviewing accounts.** Thieves go after the easy mark, and embezzlers are thieves. If you're diligent about reviewing your accounts, people are less likely to try to steal from you. And if fraud does occur, you will be able to identify and put a stop to it more quickly if you are regularly reviewing the accounts.
- **Double-check *everything*.** You have to double-check everything. You can't blindly trust that others will do their jobs honestly or correctly.
- **Look at percentages.** You should have a general idea of your gross profit margin (sales after accounting for the direct cost of producing those sales) as well as your net profit margin (your actual profit, after accounting for all costs). Once you know what the

percentages should be, you can quickly review statements and see whether the numbers are in line with your expectations. If the percentages are off, it might be due to embezzlement. Even small variances in the percentage should be investigated. Just 1% of $10 million is $100,000, and if the embezzlement is spread across many years, that amount will quickly add up.
- **Utilize good hiring practices.** Your employees form the foundation of your business, so be diligent in your background checks and verify new hires' qualifications.

FURTHER INFORMATION
- For more information on how to track and record assets, such as cash and bank accounts, see chapter 7, "Reconciling Your Accounts."

CHAPTER 3

MAKING A PROFIT

FROM REVENUE TO PROFIT—ACCURATELY TRACKING YOUR MONEY

Matthew came to eeCPA because he was disappointed with the profit his company was making. His sales had grown exponentially—he used to be doing $2 million in business a year and now was doing $12 million a year. He had a sales-tracking app on his phone, so he could see all these orders, but the corresponding profit just wasn't there. He didn't understand why, and he wanted answers to the all-important question: "Why am I not making money?"

We dived into an analysis of his financial records and discovered several issues.

The biggest issue was Matthew was working from faulty data. A system only works if you use it consistently and input data appropriately. At Matthew's company, a lot of the information wasn't being entered in the system at the right time. The most glaring of the issues was that income would be recorded as soon as an order was received but *before* the sale actually occurred. So of course Matthew thought he had more money than he really did. He was essentially counting his chickens before they hatched. He would see $10,000 worth of orders and assume that meant $10,000 of income. He didn't account for the corresponding expenses of the sale—for example, paying subcontractors, purchasing supplies, and so on.

Another issue was that Matthew's sales and expenses were being recorded on different sets of software. Even when costs were properly inputted, they were not being pulled in properly to the reports. As a result, it looked like he was making 10% profit on the sales, but in reality, his costs were much more significant, and that profit margin was much smaller.

Also, like many point-of-sale systems, Matthew's app was giving him only real-time data about what had been ordered *today*. Real-time data is fantastic, but it needs to be verified in context. For example, Matthew's app wasn't taking into account the fact that some sales were "made," but then the credit card used as payment was rejected, the order was later canceled, or the product was returned.

When we did our analysis, we discovered that more than 10% of daily sales were returned. Even though Matthew was looking at his sales reports each day, he didn't realize the return rate was so high, because that info wasn't included in his app. Not only was he making fewer sales than he realized, but he also wasn't accounting for the restocking fee associated with those returns.

Finally, we also discovered some hidden wasteful spending—namely, the company was incurring large monthly expenses of more than $1,000 for computer subscriptions that they weren't even using.

One of the first things we did was have Matthew cancel those unneeded subscriptions. Then we tweaked the system and taught his employees how to use the system properly so that Matthew would be working from accurate data. With accurate data, we were able to determine that part of the reason for the high return rate was that they were selling the wrong product much of the time. For every ten sales, one customer would be sold the wrong part and have to return it. So Matthew's sales staff needed better sales training to ensure customers got the correct products, thus reducing the number of returns.

While it was disappointing for Matthew to learn that his profit wasn't really as high as he expected, with the proper information in his pocket, he was able to make the needed changes to start raising his profit margin to where he wanted it to be.

WHY ARE YOU MAKING LESS THAN YOU EXPECT?
INACCURATE DATA

If you're working from a set of numbers that doesn't truly reflect your business's health, you may think everything is great when it isn't.

The first cause of inaccurate numbers is poor accounting processes. One major mistake is booking sales before they're confirmed. Remember, a sale is only a sale once the customer has committed to payment.

Another issue is misinterpreting or misunderstanding the numbers. For example, revenue only becomes profit once the correlated expenses have been taken care of. If you don't match revenue to costs, you won't see the full picture. Generally, you get the sale first, and then the cost of fulfillment comes second. If you're only looking at your sales and not taking into account the cost of generating and delivering on that sale, you're going to overestimate your profit.

You need to have valid, accurate information, because otherwise, how can you expect to make the right decisions for your business? If your profit is overstated, you may decide to invest in a larger space, hire a receptionist, or purchase new equipment when in reality you can't afford any of those things. Then, a few months down the line, you will find yourself in a precarious position.

AGED RECEIVABLES

Having aged receivables is an issue because the longer your receivables sit, the less likely you'll be able to collect that money. There are a number of reasons why you might not be collecting your receivables fast enough—maybe you're not getting your billing out in a timely manner, maybe your payment terms are too generous, or maybe you're not following up on late payments. At many businesses, no one has time to call and see when Johnny is going to pay his bill, but if nobody checks on receivables repeatedly and regularly, you are never going to get that money.

Your sales could be growing exponentially, but if you can't collect on those sales, then it doesn't matter. What good is it to have $200,000 in sales if all of that is uncollectable, delinquent debt sitting in accounts receivable?

OVERCOMMITMENT TO SPACE OR EMPLOYEES

Overcommitment to space or employees is a common pitfall you might run into, especially when your business is in the process of expanding.

Let's say you know you're going to double your business in the next two years. As a result, you've leased a bunch of extra space in anticipation of your business's growth. Doing so secures you the right to future expansion without having to negotiate with your landlord or potentially even move. Maybe you were able to get a good deal on the extra space too. In any case, you went ahead and signed a ten-year lease. However, for as long as that extra space is not occupied or utilized, you're incurring an extra cost that doesn't generate revenue.

You should always try to fully utilize all the assets of a business. If your business can't use it yet, can you sublet it, perhaps to a coworking space? At the very least, you should work to minimize the cost of that unused area. For example, can you turn off the utilities to that area? It's OK to purchase additional space ahead of time if you know you're going to need it soon, but you need a temporary plan in the meantime to make that space work for you.

If something goes wrong and you don't experience the expected growth, you could be SOL, stuck with a large space hemorrhaging money you can't afford to lose. So you should only enter into a lease for such a space if you have some kind of plan for how to use the space until you need it.

Just as many businesses commit to too much space, many businesses also hire new employees before they can truly afford them. Let's say you don't have the time anymore to answer the phone, so you're considering hiring a receptionist, which can be a significant expense. Let's say you get five calls a day. With an eight-hour day at $15 an hour, a receptionist costs you a total of $120, or about $25 per call. And that's not even factoring in all the other expenses of an employee besides their wage. If those calls are needed for customer care, then you can still go ahead and hire the receptionist. However, you need to factor the receptionist's wage into your cost of doing business and ensure you will still have a high enough profit margin.

You also need to make sure your employees have enough work to do. If that receptionist is taking only five calls a day, they will have a lot of down time. What else can you give them to do to ensure productivity?

HIDDEN WASTEFUL SPENDING AND COSTS

It can be hard to determine what is wasteful spending, especially without a forecast or budget, as there are so many ways to waste money. For example, just in booking flights, five different people on your team could come up with five different prices for a flight, because they're focused on different things. One person might always choose the same airline, because they like that airline. Another might be focused on the time of the flight. Yet another employee might be focused on the cheapest flight, but maybe that ends up requiring double the flight time and incurring other kinds of expenses.

Sometimes you waste money by paying more than is needed for an item, like a flight ticket in this example. You should always explore and price the different options to get the best deal. You should also set company policies for employee spending before the spending occurs. For example, for travel costs, you could establish a preferred hotel chain and set desired cost parameters, such as $100 a night for hotels and $500 or less for domestic airline tickets.

Other times wasteful spending occurs because you're paying for something you don't need. Look at all the various subscriptions you have, such as software subscriptions. Are you utilizing all of them? You might have other assets not being fully utilized as well. For example, maybe your printers keep breaking, so you buy ten to have backups. Do you need that many backups? Maybe just one or two would be enough. How about ink cartridges? How many do you really need for your printers? Do you need to have five in surplus, or can you live with three?

Try to be lean in your business. The more surplus and backups you keep on hand, then the more assets you have to manage and keep track of. Instead of tying your capital up in supplies you won't need for a while, hold on to your cash to increase your spending options.

You could also be wasting money if you're not assessing your ROI. A lot of times, people pour money into marketing and assume it is working without ever analyzing the numbers. Let's say you put $2,500 into a new marketing program. OK, so how many leads did you get this month from that initiative? Maybe you find you're getting only ten leads a month. That comes out to $250 per lead. If you weren't planning on spending that much per lead, then maybe this wasn't the right solution for you.

The last common type of hidden wasteful spending is unexpected product cost increases. Sometimes your vendor won't communicate cost increases to you right away, and you could end up paying a higher price for your supplies without accounting for the increase in your cost of fulfillment, slashing your profit margin. This is one of the reasons you absolutely need to know what your gross profit margin should be and what it actually is, so you can quickly identify when something has changed.

OTHER REASONS YOU MIGHT BE MAKING LESS PROFIT THAN PLANNED

NOT HAVING A PLAN OR HAVING TOO MANY PLANS

If you don't have a plan or process, your profits will likely be lower than expected, but if you try to implement too many plans at once, you also might end up with disappointing profits. If you make too many changes in your business at one time, you will lose sight of the big picture, and you won't understand the impact of all the individual changes.

I fell into this trap in 2017. My company hired a PR firm in July, we outsourced our SEO in August, and then I signed the contract for publishing this book in October. We had $5,000 a month allocated for the book, $2,500 for the SEO person, and then another $2,000 for the PR person—almost $10,000 total, with no way to track the impact of each individual investment. While all this was happening, we were also in the middle of moving into a new office space. We had bitten off quite a bit more than we could chew.

We had the money earmarked in our budget, but we did things in the wrong sequence. For example, we didn't have enough new events to publicize to justify the PR person, who would really be most helpful *after* the book was released. Plus, we had outsourced to two different firms for the PR and SEO, and they weren't working together cohesively.

When you're caught up in the momentum of your business, it is easy to get carried away, but you must strategize your hiring and outsourcing process not only in conjunction with your budget but also in terms of effectiveness. Ask yourself, "Does it make sense to do x, y, and z all at once, or should I be doing them one at a time?"

In my case, we should have started with the SEO, gone ahead with the book, and then introduced the PR about six months later when the book was published and there was more to publicize. At the very least, we should have waited until our building move was finalized. It took me six months to realize I had hired the PR person at the wrong time, and so we wasted $2,000 a month for six months. That $12,000 could have been profit had I focused on doing just one thing at a time.

So you might have a plan and the budget for something, but timing is key. Just because you have the money available doesn't mean you have to spend it if it's not the right time. Make the best use of your resources at the right time, whether that's money invested into marketing, the amount of space you lease, or the number of people you employ.

Approach changes from an analytical perspective, kind of like the scientific method. If you change two variables at the same time, you won't know which one drove the most impact, especially when it comes to marketing and things where the link between cause and effect isn't always obvious. Instead, develop a hypothesis—a forecast of the expected effect—and then perform the experiment. Take the time to explore one change at a time, so that you know what works and what doesn't. Constantly reevaluate what your ROI is.

So have a plan, but keep changes down to one variable when possible.

NOT UNDERSTANDING HOW THINGS WORK

I have several clients who try to do things on their own to save money on fees but still bring me in for audits. I'm always happy to help my clients in whatever way I can, but in trying to save money on fees, many of these clients make costly mistakes. They don't fully understand how things work, so they can't identify issues.

In one example, I had a client who wanted to move $76,000 from one account to another account and submitted the request to Nationwide. Nationwide said they didn't have clear enough instructions to make the transfer, so the client canceled the request.

Then a year and a half later, in 2017, we were doing an audit of the client's entire plan, reviewing and verifying all the accounts. At this point, we determined that the $76,000 had indeed left the first account but had never been placed into the second account. We launched an investigation and discovered that Nationwide had temporarily "lost" the money.

After many back-and-forth phone calls and emails, Nationwide found the money and replaced the funds. But meanwhile that money had been missing from this client's account for almost two years by that point—two years when the money could have been working for him but wasn't. So even though he got the money back, he still lost out on the opportunity cost of using the money for the past two years. He also told us he never would have noticed the money was missing on his own, so if it weren't for our audit and verification process, he would have lost the $76,000 altogether.

Double-check, double-check, double-check! I've said it already, and I'll say it again. There are so many mistakes that can be avoided by double-checking. Even if you give instructions in writing, you must verify that your instructions are carried out properly.

As another example, let's say you enter into a contract for new phone services, and instead of turning the contract over to your accounting or finance team, you file it away in a drawer. Then, when the invoice comes in a month later, it's for double the agreed-upon price in your contract, which happens way more often than you'd think. If you don't have an approval or verification process in your company, then you might end up paying more than the contracted rate and never realizing it. Instead of being kept in a random drawer or file, the phone contract should be attached directly to the transaction so that the rate can be verified.

You need to follow every transaction through from beginning to end—from contract to payment—and verify all the pieces every single time. Watch out for inconsistencies. Otherwise, you could wind up paying way more for certain services or products, just because you don't have an approval process in place or some kind of notification for inconsistencies.

PRACTICES TO INCREASE PROFIT
ESTABLISH A PLAN

The best way you can increase your profit is to make a budget. The word *budget* scares some people, so think of it more as a forecast or a plan. You should know your expected revenue, expected costs, and thus expected net profit. For example, maybe you plan to do $2 million in business, expect to spend $1.5 million on costs, and thus expect your net profit to be $500,000.

From there, you don't need to budget out every little thing, such as how much you're going to spend on pencils and paper, but you should have an overall plan of how much you're going to spend in all the different buckets of expenses. How much is your rent? How much is the cost of your employees at their current salaried rates? How much do you spend on average per year for supplies?

You have to have a baseline. Then you have to track what is actually happening against that baseline. If you plan to spend $100,000 for the year and find you've already spent $50,000 by the end of February, you need to replan.

Maybe you plan to have ten full-time employees, each making $10,000 a month. What if one of those people doesn't work out, and you hire two part-time people instead? What if you give one or more employees a raise? Now all of a sudden, the salaries are coming in over budget by $20,000 a month. Where's that $20,000 going to come from? If you aren't actively comparing the actual numbers with the forecasted numbers, you won't identify and account for all these moving pieces of the puzzle. That means that $20,000 is going to come from the bottom line—from your profit. If you were expecting to make $500,000 this year, you're now down to just $260,000 because you're spending $20,000 more per month than you anticipated.

You have to constantly look at your budget as a moving

target and watch it every single month. If you look at it only at the end of the year, it is too late. You will have already spent the money, and there is no way to get it back. If you check your budget regularly, you can adjust and make cuts in other areas to keep your bottom line on target, as originally planned.

Make the plan. Compare the plan against the reality. Then make decisions based on that information and adjust the plan to keep your profit steady.

KEEP IT SIMPLE

You need to keep your budget as simple as possible, as this allows you the most flexibility to make changes and to see patterns more readily. If you have thousands of charts in a six-page-long report, there are too many numbers for you to process and factor into your decisions. It is simply too overwhelming. For businesses with less than $1 million in revenue, your budget report should be just one page long, two max, covering just the five or six largest categories.

Start with the big picture, and then once you identify important trends, you can break things down to greater detail. So on your P&L, I recommend listing out income, direct costs, sales and marketing costs, payroll costs, general and administrative costs, and occupancy costs.

Looking at this summary, perhaps you discover that you're off budget for direct costs. Then you can drill down in detail and look at individual transactions within direct costs to find out where you are off plan. Then you can begin making decisions about how to fix the problem. Without first looking at the large trends, you might not have realized that direct costs were the problem, and so you never would have been able to identify and fix the issue.

You should also choose software that's easy for you and your team to use. There are so many different products in the marketplace, but the simpler the system is and the easier it is to find and enter information into the system, the more likely it is that you and your employees will actually use the software.

Simple and easy also equals fewer errors. If your software requires a lot of clicks, sending you into a seemingly never-ending abyss of submenus to find or enter data, then the learning curve for that software will be high, with a far more substantial risk of incorrect information being entered. Inaccurate data will do you more harm than good.

Setting up a simple, easy system is one of my main goals with every client but especially for my cannabis clients. Because marijuana is still listed as a Schedule I drug, it is illegal federally even when it is legal within a particular state. Most banking institutions rely heavily on the federal government, so most marijuana businesses do not have easy access to bank accounts. As a result, they are incredibly cash-intensive businesses, and it is imperative to find a way for them to track all the cash, as there is no ledger or bank account to record that information for them.

For one of eeCPA's cannabis clients, our solution came in the form of a smartphone app called Receipt Bank. All employees have to do is download the app on their smartphones and take pictures of all the expense receipts. The pictures are uploaded to a cloud-based dashboard, and the needed data—vendor names, dollar amounts, and the like—is automatically pulled from the receipt and populated into the system. Now the business has a paper trail. Because the app is so simple to use for the end user, the data is very accurate.

At this point, we, as the accounting firm, can go into the app and review and encode every receipt. We can then import all this information into our QuickBooks Online accounting software, and every transaction will have the original receipt attached to it. If there's ever a question, such as why they bought ten vape pens, we can go back and see who purchased the vape pens, when they purchased them, what supplier they purchased them from, and how much they paid.

This app has been so successful for our cannabis clients that I now use it for my firm and recommend it even to clients who are not in the cannabis industry. There's no rummaging through a shoebox of receipts or searching through file folders to try to find a needed receipt. Instead, you just pull up the transaction in the accounting system, and everything—all the details and source documentation related to that transaction—is right there, at the click of a mouse.

DOCUMENT YOUR PROCESS

Every year I have a client who says, "We talked about this last year, but I don't remember—how are we recording sales?" You might think you will remember everything, but chances are, you won't. So you need to document your process for future reference.

For eeCPA as well as our clients, we use another app for this: Process Street. Whereas before you might have had a handful of different Microsoft Word and PDF how-to guides saved everywhere, with Process Street, you can document all the processes for your businesses in one place. With this app, you can create different tasks, and you can link tasks together so that task 1 must be completed before task 2 and so on. Then you can assign people to the various steps, and when they open up the app, they see all the tasks they must complete that day or week right there. Tasks don't disappear from an employee's checklist until they're completed and some tasks can't be checked off until prerequisite tasks are completed, so nothing gets missed.

When we take on a new client at eeCPA, we completely set up a customized accounting system and process for them within this app. So let's say Sue is a new client. We set up a daily process for her to run Monday through Friday. All she needs to do is open up the app, and then she goes through and checks off each task in her daily process as she completes it. So once she records transactions from the bank account and matches them to the actual transactions, for example, she checks off that item. Then at the end of each month, additional checklists will pop up in the app for her to close out the prior month. These tasks will include things such as reconciling the bank and credit card accounts and reviewing how revenue has been recorded. All these various checklists are saved within the app, so you don't need to reinvent the wheel each time.

In addition to being easy, this process is incredibly transparent as well. You can see exactly which steps have been completed and which haven't, and you can see who completed various steps and when, down to the exact minute even. This app is an excellent training tool for new hires as well as an ongoing tool to double-check and make sure you don't miss any of the steps. This ensures financial statements are as correct as they can be.

THINK ABOUT OUTSOURCING

Most people have a payroll company, a bookkeeper, a CPA, a third-party administrator, and maybe even a tax attorney. When you outsource all those different functions to different people, that's four, five, or even more different people whom you have to coordinate. None of these people work with the other people, so you're in charge of making sure the right information gets to the right people. You have to make sure that that payroll information gets to your bookkeeper. Then you have to make sure your bookkeeper's compiled data gets to the CPA. Then you have to get the CPA's financial employment data to the retirement plan provider. And on and on and on. It's like trying to wrangle cats. Outsourcing all your various accounting functions to a single firm instead can save money and increase profit.

In hindsight, I certainly wish I had outsourced to a single do-it-all firm when eeCPA was building our new space. Instead, I had a separate contractor, designer, and architect. Then the contractor said the architect's drawings weren't good enough, so I hired another architect to supplement the first architect. Then that new architect hired an engineer. Then the contractor said they couldn't follow the engineer's drawings, so I hired another engineer.

Meanwhile, I'd been promised that my building project would be done in ten weeks, and we were now at week fifteen. The project still wasn't done, and my herd of cats to wrangle just kept getting larger. It was an expensive project, and I was—understandably, I would say—getting frustrated. Nobody was taking responsibility because they all had someone else to point the finger at. The contractor said, "It's the architect." The architect said, "No, it's the engineer." And so on.

I wasted so much time trying to track down who gave what instruction to whom to find out why the project was not progressing at the promised rate. At the end of the day, I wasn't getting what I wanted, but I had no recourse. I couldn't prove any one party was more at fault than another, so I was trapped. I couldn't get my money back or force them to deliver service by the agreed-upon time. In total, the work ended up taking more than twenty weeks—twice as long as quoted.

If I could do it over, I would have hired just one company to do it all—the architecture, design, and construction. Then, if the contracted work was not completed as specified, instead of finger-pointing, there would have been accountability, and I would have had recourse.

Having a single firm handling all your accounting needs can also save you money. First and foremost, you will save time and thus money by not having to coordinate all the various pieces. Also, instead of having to hire several different people at their full rates, you can get all the services you need at a discounted packaged rate.

Outsourcing to a single firm also provides stability, not only because there is accountability for the work but also because you no longer have to worry about employment issues. You don't have to worry about sick employees, vacation time, the hiring process, or raises, because you're contracting with a firm and they're guaranteeing to have somebody in place, on time, with the right information and knowledge to complete the job for you.

Do-it-all firms also have more resources to leverage than individuals. For example, we had a client at eeCPA where we were only contracted to do their tax work. They had their own in-house bookkeeper who did all their sales tax filings and coordinated their payroll services. Then one day, we got a call from them because they'd gotten a bank levy from the Arizona Department of Revenue for outstanding sales tax. The bookkeeper hadn't been keeping up to date with current sales tax regulations, resulting in reporting errors that had led to this sudden levy of about $48,500.

The company didn't have those funds available, as they needed the money to cover their payroll, so we had to make an emergency appeal with the state government to release the levies. To get the levy released, the client had to provide sixteen months of corrected sales tax reports, which took quite a bit of work. We were able to get all that money back for them, but it cost them a few thousand dollars of our time. They didn't have the money for ten days, and they were understandably stressed over it, as well as embarrassed, because all their banks (with whom they had lines of credit) had received the levy notices and expressed concern.

You need to have the right people in the right seats to guarantee good work. At eeCPA, we have a variety of specialists we can leverage in any given situation, and we stay up to date on the tax legislation for every state. If this client had hired us for all his accounting needs, he wouldn't have had his accounts levied, and he wouldn't have gone through all that stress either. Or if an error *had* still occurred for any reason, we guarantee our work, so he wouldn't be paying our fee.

When it comes to choosing a company to work with, focus on these questions: Do they have the relevant expertise that you need? What is their reputation in the community? Have they been in business for a long time? Are they insured and bonded to protect against fraud? What is their process for hiring employees? Do they guarantee their services?

To give you an idea of what you should be looking for, at eeCPA, we do thorough background checks on all our employees for criminal activity, driver's license verification, drug testing, degree verification, and licensure verification. We also do credit checks to make sure they're honoring their debts. We will not hire anyone that has ever claimed bankruptcy. We also have employee dishonesty coverage and other insurance coverage that our clients can make claims against, so if there is an issue, they have recourse. Plus, we have someone available 24-7 to address any concerns a client may have.

So with outsourcing, the benefits are that you get one point of contact, you have recourse if something goes wrong, you can save money by bundling services, and you have a service guarantee.

KEY TIPS

- **If it's easy, you'll do it.** There are so many little things to keep track of, so you have to keep this easy.
- **Less is more.** When it comes to your accounting system and processes, less is more. The fewer moving parts you have, the easier the system is to manage, and the better chance you have of achieving a positive result. Concentrate on the big stuff.
- **Focus on profit, not revenue.** Most entrepreneurs are naturally focused on sales—they may even get

daily updates about sales—but they don't always take the next step to profit. Get a monthly report of what is going on with your business that includes not only the sales but also the big buckets of expenses. Then focus on that all-important profit number.

- **Make a plan, compare the reality to the plan, and adjust.** Make a plan, even if it's on the back of a napkin. Then check how reality compares to that plan every single month, adjusting as needed.
- **Consider outsourcing your accounting work.** Outsourcing can save you money while getting you top-notch talent. If you outsource, make sure to contract with a company that offers a service guarantee.

FURTHER INFORMATION

- For more information on the profit and loss statement, the key report to show you your revenue and expenses, see chapters 11–14.

CHAPTER 4

STAYING OUT OF DEBT

LIFE TURNED UPSIDE DOWN—DEBILITATING DEBT

More than 20% of businesses fail in the first year. By five years, around *half* of businesses close their doors, and only about a third make it past the ten-year mark.[4] One of the biggest reasons? They simply run out of money, often due to debt. Debt is a huge obstacle to overcome in business—one that my client Robert has unfortunately found himself facing.

To fund his solar business, Robert used several credit card accounts—seven, in fact—along with credit from his vendors. Like many business owners, he had a book-

---

[4] US Bureau of Labor Statistics, "Chart 3: Survival Rates of Establishments, by Year Started and Number of Years since Starting, 1994-2015, in Percent," last modified April 28, 2016, https://www.bls.gov/bdm/entrepreneurship/bdm_chart3.htm.

keeper whom he loved. She came to work every day and seemed reliable and skilled. He also had an outsourced CFO who came in one day a week. The CFO was modernizing the accounting system, moving the whole system from one platform to another. When he came in each week, he would give the bookkeeper a to-do list of data that needed to be reentered into the new system. The bookkeeper soon became overwhelmed because in addition to keeping the books, she had to answer the phone, help with other administrative tasks, and now reenter all this data.

While the bookkeeper was falling more and more behind, Robert continued receiving financial statements each month that made it seem like he was making tons of money. He was working on getting all his credit cards paid off, and he felt like the business was in a great place. Based on the positive numbers of growth he was seeing, he even made moves to expand. He hired new team members, pursued more advertising, and invested in new equipment.

Then one day Robert got a call from one of his vendors saying, "You owe us $250,000 for solar panels."

It was like a bucket of ice water to the face. Robert didn't have $250,000 just lying around. *How could this have happened?* he wondered.

With some investigation, Robert discovered that his bookkeeper had gotten so far behind that she hadn't entered any of the vendor invoices into their system for *months*. All the invoices were just sitting in a drawer. Because the invoices had never been entered in the system, none of those costs were recognized on the profit and loss statement, resulting in the vastly overstated profit numbers Robert had been working from for several months.

At this point, Robert fired both his CFO and bookkeeper. Neither the CFO nor the bookkeeper had malicious intent, but their ineptitude had cost Robert dearly. The bookkeeper only had the skills to enter data; she didn't know how to analyze what the various financial statements said and didn't understand how they corresponded back to the data she entered. On the CFO's part, he was completely sidetracked by his mission to rebuild a new, better system for tracking costs and somehow failed to notice that the very thing he was trying to track wasn't being updated in the system.

It was a calamity of errors, and because there was no double-checking system in place—no checks and balances, no definite policies and procedures—no one noticed anything until the vendor called. Robert had made the mistake of implicitly trusting the "professionals" he'd hired. He wasn't asking questions or double-checking, so everything fell through the cracks.

Left to pick up the pieces, Robert went back to his old accounting system and started all over again. With a new, accurate set of numbers finally in hand and a mountain of debt to overcome, he was forced to radically change his entire business. He also had to let half of his team go because he didn't have the money he thought he did to pay them.

Robert discovered this debt about a year and a half ago, and he's still struggling to overcome it. For a year and a half, he has not been able to cut a paycheck for himself out of his business. His wife, who had been a stay-at-home mom, had to go back to work. His kids' lives have been turned upside down too. Robert is now the one to pick them up from school because his wife is back at work. Many days, he takes them on sales calls with him. He can't leave them home alone and can't afford a sitter, but he must continue to drive sales to keep the business afloat. At this point, it is borderline whether his business will survive this setback or become just another statistic.

BIGGEST CAUSES OF DEBT
NOT PUTTING BILLS IN THE SYSTEM

The biggest cause of debt is not putting bills into the system, and it happens all the time.

One of the main reasons bills don't make it into the

system is exactly what happened to Robert: there is a young woman acting as bookkeeper/receptionist/general office administrator. She is in charge of a dozen different things, and paying the bills is last on the list. So when she gets overwhelmed, the bills fall by the wayside.

When the bills aren't in the system, there is no way for you to have an accurate pulse on your business's health and financial obligations.

HOLDING CHECKS

Another easy way to fall into debt is holding checks—you properly input the bill into the system and then cut the check to pay it, but you don't have enough money in your account to cover the check, so you hold on to the check for days or weeks, not sending it until the needed funds become available.

I have one client who was notorious for doing this. As a result, their financial numbers would be wildly inaccurate. In reality, they might have $15,000 in their bank account and $135,000 in payables, but they would go ahead and cut checks for $115,000 worth of their payables. Thus, according to their financial reports, it would look like they had just $20,000 in payables, and the bank account would appear to be overdrawn by $100,000, which is of course impossible. Then, once they received a payment from a customer, say worth $200,000, their bank account would be replenished, and they would finally send out the checks they'd already cut.

By doing it this way, if a vendor called to ask about payment, someone could look in the system and say, "We cut a check on January 2. You should receive it any day now." While they could honestly say they'd cut the check, it was basically a big sham, because they didn't have the money in the account to cover the check and hadn't really sent it out yet.

It's tough to plan for settlement with vendors if you frequently hold checks, as it is difficult to figure out what is owed. The only way to know how much you owe and how much cash you actually have is to rifle through the drawer and manually add up all the checks to see what has been mailed out and what hasn't. Instead of writing checks and then holding on to them, you should wait until you have the money in your account to cover the checks and *then* cut the checks. That way your financial statements will be correct at all times throughout the process and will accurately reflect your true cash reserves.

COMINGLING FUNDS

The next major cause of debt is comingling funds.

A lot of entrepreneurs put money into their businesses

from personal sources—for example, family loans, home equity lines, and so on—to get started. But they never put the seed money on the books to show that, say, they borrowed $25,000 from their personal line of credit to start up the business. By failing to properly record your seed money, you lose the tax benefits of all that money, and you obviously must not have a good plan to pay it back, because it's not even recognized as a debt on the company's books. The money disappears into thin air, with no evidence of it anywhere in your accounting or general ledger.

The second you comingle personal and business funds, you're bound to lose track of important initial investments. The day you open your business, you should open a business banking account. Deposit any and all investments and seed money into that account, even if you're borrowing from your line of credit. Then spend out of that account. Doing this will create a trail showing the deposits and will ensure that all personal investments and seed money spent on the business are recorded and can thus be paid back someday.

FORGETTING ABOUT CREDIT CARD EXPENDITURES

The last major cause of debt is a failure to incorporate credit card expenditures into the accounting system.

It is so easy to charge something and forget about it. Just swipe and you're done. If you forget to transfer those transactions over to your general ledger, though, it will look like you're making a profit when you're not. You could have a $100,000 debt sitting unnoticed right under your nose.

It is especially important to track credit card debt because the interest rates are so high. Whenever it is possible, don't finance your business with credit cards. There are more cost-effective options available to you, such as opening up a line of credit with your bank.

UPSIDE-DOWN PROFIT: YOU'RE GENERATING PROFIT BUT HAVE NO CASH

Upside-down profit is when it appears you have made a profit on paper but are cash poor. Upside-down profit often becomes an issue when tax time rolls around and you suddenly owe tens of thousands of dollars in taxes and have no cash to cover the payment.

The biggest cause of upside-down profit is having too much debt that isn't properly recorded. Upside-down profit is a major concern for business owners just starting out, but it can also occur later on in the business's life, when you take out credit to buy new equipment, to fund a new division, or to invest in other types of expansion.

You need to record the total amount of your debt on the books. Don't just record the payments you're making toward the debt. If you don't properly record the full amount of debt, you might be showing a profit, but in reality, all that money is going to paying back the debt.

Also, if you carry debt forward from year to year, it might not be a tax deduction anymore; it might be accumulated debt. Say you buy a new $100,000 truck on credit on December 31, 2017, and choose to expense 100% of it to lower your 2017 taxes. Then, in 2018, when you actually start paying off the truck, you won't get to deduct any of those payments as expenses, as you already deducted the full value of the truck; you will only be able to deduct the interest. When you make the debt payments in this case, they won't show up on the profit and loss statement, because they're a liability you're paying off. So when taxes come due, you might not have enough cash to pay the bill, as all that cash went to repaying old debt.

In my opinion, it is always best to take advantage of all tax deductions and then simply plan ahead for the debt repayment, provided that the acquisition is business critical and not merely a strategy to get the tax deduction!

You also might fall into the trap of upside-down profit if you're on the accrual system of accounting and expense items before actually paying for them. Because the money hasn't left your account yet, it can show up as available cash on your reports. Later, when you're stuck actually paying for the expensed items as well as taxes, you might find yourself coming up short.

Upside-down profit is also commonly caused by booking sales before the expenses associated with the sale have been fully recognized or by having outstanding accounts receivable. Many businesses will get a deposit from a customer and book the sale, but it might be several months before the product or service is actually delivered and the balance of payment is received. Thus, it looks like the business has more money than it actually does because the sale was booked before it was truly completed.

Repaying debt is of course important, but you need to ensure debt repayment doesn't come at the cost of sacrificing your business's cash flow. Therefore, you need to plan ahead and properly come up with a cash-flow plan that includes a plan for debt repayment.

PRACTICES TO HELP THE CASH FLOW OF YOUR BUSINESS

PUT ALL ACCOUNTS ON THE BALANCE SHEET

Putting all accounts on the balance sheet, including all debts and accounts payable, is absolutely critical. Also, be sure to pull in data from credit card purchases.

If you record bills only when you pay them, you will have an inaccurate picture of your business's financial health. You will also forget what bills are still outstanding if you don't keep track. So record bills and debts as soon as they're incurred.

Periodically verify the numbers of all liabilities and double-check the balances to ensure everything is accurate.

BE CLEAR ABOUT HOW LIABILITIES ARE REPORTED

Some liabilities are due right away, and others are not. Current liabilities are liabilities that are due within the next year, such as payroll taxes or vendor invoices. Longer-term liabilities are liabilities that are not due within the next year, such as installment loans where you have five years or more to repay them. On a five-year loan, only one year's worth of payments is considered a current liability, and the remaining four years' payments are long-term liabilities.

You need to clearly identify and record what is a current liability and what is a long-term liability. A current liability requires immediate cash, and repaying that debt within the year needs to be a part of your financial plan. However, you might be able to refinance a long-term liability. For example, you could refinance a five-year loan to spread out the payments over ten years. You can even refinance and consolidate credit card debt. But until you know which liabilities are current and which are long term, it is hard to come up with a plan to refinance or restructure.

PRIORITIZE DEBTS

If you don't have all the money you need to pay all your bills, you will have to prioritize certain debts.

For example, let's say you're in a tight spot temporarily. You have a big customer payment coming in next week, but before that comes in, you have two bills due this week and can afford to pay only one. One bill is for your utilities, and one is with your vendor Joe, whom you have a strong relationship with.

If you don't pay your utility bill this week, you're not going to have lights on in your office next week. However, because you have a good relationship with Joe, you know he'll be willing to give you an extension and accept payment the following week. So in this case, it would make sense to prioritize the utility bill payment and then pay Joe the following week.

DEVELOP GOOD RELATIONSHIPS WITH YOUR VENDORS

Work to develop good relationships with your vendors early on. Sometimes you might not be able to pay your vendors immediately because you have to pay taxes or some other debt instead. In this situation, many people go radio silent. They stop responding to vendor inquiries about due payments and try to ignore the problem.

The problem won't go away, though; it is only going to get bigger. If your vendors aren't getting paid and you don't open the lines of communication, your vendors will start to get angry and will cut you off. Many industries are tight-knit, so if you burn your bridges with one vendor, you could get blackballed in the entire industry and won't be able to get your needed supplies from anyone. If you can't get the supplies you need to fulfill your sales, your entire operation will be affected, and it will be that much more difficult to pay back your debts. In extreme cases, your vendors might serve liens or levies against your property or other assets. They might even file lawsuits.

If you don't have your vendors on your side, debt can easily send your business into bankruptcy. So if you cannot pay a vendor right away, it is better to be proactive. Reach out as soon as you know there is an issue. Explain the situation and make arrangements to pay them back over time. That last part is key. Vendors have heard lots of sob stories about why people can't pay and are largely immune to such emotional pleas, but if you take the initiative to formulate a plan of repayment, vendors will be more likely to work with you, ensuring you can keep getting supplies and making sales.

WHAT IF YOU ARE ALREADY IN OVER YOUR HEAD?
COME UP WITH A REPAYMENT PLAN

If you're already in debt, you need to come up with a payment restructuring plan. Identify everything that is owed, refinance debt where possible, and then contact each vendor or creditor (including the government) to come up with a repayment plan.

Even if you owe taxes, you have so many options available to you. You can do installment payment agreements, spreading out the balance you owe over several years, and you can also take advantage of an offer in compromise, where the government agrees to accept less than the full payment in settlement of the outstanding balance owed.

DO FINANCIAL MODELING

If you want to refinance your debt, you will likely need to do financial modeling, to show that your business can be profitable at some point in the future. If you can't show banks and other institutions that your business can be a success, they won't want to take on your debt.

SEEK A CONSULTANT

If you're overwhelmed by debt, you need a consultant. Few people who get stuck in this situation are able to dig themselves out all on their own. If you hire a consultant, you will have an expert in your corner who can evaluate the state of your business and advise you on next steps. They can help you set up a proper accounting system so that you don't run into the same financial problems again, and they can also negotiate with your vendors to form repayment plans.

SECURE ADDITIONAL FUNDING

Issues with debt often result in a direct hit to your pocket, as the business owner. You're likely going to have to come up with more money on your own. Your other option is to find someone else who is willing to invest in your business, which is hard to do if you're already in debt. But it is possible to find people who are willing to partner with you, especially if you offer a very attractive package to your potential partner.

If things are bleak and you can't secure additional funding, you may end up having to close your doors or file a

Chapter 11 bankruptcy reorganization to try to stave off your creditors.

REBUILD RELATIONSHIPS

Nobody likes not getting paid, so you will have to put time and effort into rebuilding trust and repairing your business relationships that have been affected by your debt. Debt can even damage relationships irreparably, forcing you to find entirely new vendors and consultants and build new relationships.

BE PROACTIVE

The faster and more proactive you are in identifying and addressing a problem, the more options you have. The longer you let things go without taking action, the worse the problem becomes. Debt is scary, but if you ignore it or try to deny it, then it's going to continue to snowball, risking the permanent closure of your business. Instead, admit that you've made some mistakes and take immediate action. The faster you act, the better chance your business has of overcoming the debt.

KEY TIPS

- **Record all debts in your accounting system.** To ensure an accurate financial picture of your business,

you must have all debts and liabilities recorded in your accounting system.
- **Keep a copy of every receipt or invoice.** Directly attach a copy of every receipt and invoice to the relevant transaction in your accounting system. This way, if you have questions at any point, it is easy to go back and find the original documentation to verify balances. Many people choose to scan their receipts and invoices, but I recommend using an app such as Receipt Bank, where you simply need to take a picture of the receipt or invoice and then the information automatically populates.
- **Have a schedule.** You should have a schedule for everything so that things aren't pushed off for days, weeks, or even months, resulting in inaccurate profit numbers. Imagine how much better things would have turned out for Robert, from the beginning story of the chapter, if he'd designated a schedule for his bookkeeper where every bill had to be entered into the system each Friday, come hell or high water. He wouldn't have overestimated his profit so greatly, and he wouldn't have invested so much money into growth and expansion while a hidden debt was growing larger and larger in his bookkeeper's desk drawer.
- **Have a notification system for when the schedule isn't kept.** Having a notification system prevents things from falling through the cracks. In Robert's case, if he had a notification system in place, he

would have been notified the very first week that bills weren't entered as scheduled on Friday, instead of finding out several months later that there was a stack of bills that had never been inputted into the system. If something is supposed to be done by x date and isn't, either you or someone else should be notified.

- **Set up electronic approvals for payments.** Have an approval system where, once employees record and initiate a payment, someone in higher management must approve the payment. This approval process helps prevent potential fraud and embezzlement, ensuring that employees can't misuse company funds or pay their personal bills, and it also helps in the management of debt. If you're in a place where you need to prioritize certain debts over others, the approval process will ensure that instead of automatically paying whatever bill happens to come in first, you can instead pay the debts of highest priority—those debts that can't be negotiated (for example, utilities).

FURTHER INFORMATION

- To learn more about determining the amount of cash your business has, see chapter 7, "Reconciling Your Accounts."
- To learn more about how to properly record and track your debts, see chapter 9, "Cutting Your Losses."

CHAPTER 5

BUYING OR SELLING A BUSINESS

$650,000 PRICE CUT—A GOOD BUSINESS WITH BAD BOOKS

My client Jim sells custom plumbing parts—fixtures, bathtubs, toilets, faucets, and so on. He's been in business for more than twenty years and does several million dollars in sales each year. His business is successful because he knows everything there is to know about plumbing. He's never given much attention to the accounting of his business, though, leaving his books in a mess.

For the last several years, he's hired eeCPA to do his annual accounting and tax return. Each year, we've informed him that his books are a mess, but he never fixes them. So each year, we raise our fees and do some heavy-duty work to get his books into shape and make them correct for the financial statements. We essentially have to reinvent the wheel each year to figure out what his actual taxable profits are. His accounts receivable and payable logs are filled with a whole bunch of junk, such as bills that aren't really due and improperly recorded sales he never corrects.

Now Jim wants to sell his business, and all the issues he's managed to shove out of sight are going to come out of the woodwork.

His business does about $1.8 million in sales a year, and he wants to set $1.8 million as his selling price. Unfortunately, because his business is a mess from an accounting perspective, that price won't hold up in the due diligence process that occurs in any sale of a business.

First, a lot of Jim's receivables are very old and not likely to be collectable, so they're not a true asset to the business. He technically has $500,000 in receivables, but only about $100,000 of that is likely to be collected. So there's $400,000 off the selling price right there. We're down to $1.4 million.

In addition, fixtures change over time and become obsolete, so a decent chunk of his inventory is no longer salable. We've been asking him for years to take a physical inventory and to get rid of the items that aren't salable anymore, but he hasn't done that. So he may have $250,000 of inventory on the books, but in reality maybe only $100,000 of it is salable. That's another $150,000 taken off his desired selling price, taking it down to $1.25 million.

Then we get to the payables. He has a bunch of unused credits from suppliers, but those credits were issued more than three years ago and are probably not realistically redeemable anymore. So that's going to be another $100,000 off the selling price. Now we're down to $1.15 million.

All told, because of various accounting issues, Jim's business is worth $650,000 less than he thinks it's worth. That is a price cut of more than one-third.

His asking price is not likely to hold. In reality, he's probably going to get more like $1 million for his business—if he doesn't fix these issues. If he instead decides to keep the business one more year and make a plan to tidy up the books, he could get a lot closer to his asking price of $1.8 million.

With just one year of hard work, he could get a clean accounting system in place and ensure that the receivables ledger matches what's actually collectable and that the payables ledger matches what he really owes. He could also use this time to take advantage of vendor credits. By buying from vendors he has credits with, he could maximize profits and improve his bottom line. Next, he could show that he has collectable receivables, valid and salable inventory, and fewer accounts payable than it currently appears. These changes would make his business look much better to potential buyers.

If he doesn't make any of these changes and tries to proceed with a sale anyway, he's going to get killed in the due diligence process. Based on just the cold, hard math, his asking price will get slashed. But if you also consider the human factor, if Jim tries to push the sale through as is, the buyer is likely going to lose faith in him as the seller because his asking price is clearly too high and requires substantial adjustments. Many buyers would rather walk away from the sale at that point.

I've told Jim the same thing I would tell any client in this situation: if you want to get the most for your business, you absolutely must get your books in shape first.

WHY DO OWNERS OFTEN MAKE LESS ON A BUSINESS SALE THAN THEY HOPE?

The number one reason business owners make less on a

business sale than they hope is that they overvalue their business's worth. You might feel your business is worth a certain amount, but it is only worth what a buyer is willing to pay for it.

One of the reasons for this overvaluation is that business owners think the business will sell based on revenue, but it is profit, not revenue, that proves the concept of a business. Anyone can generate sales, but if the business's expenses are greater than the sales, then it is not actually a business, because it is not generating a profit.

Buyers are investors. They want a return on their investment. Typically, buyers are willing to pay only two to three times a business's yearly profit, as they want to be able to get their money back in about three years.

If you make $1.8 million in revenue, with yearly profits of $200,000, you might hope to get $1.8 million for your business, but the realistic price is a lot closer to $600,000 (three times $200,000). To get a price of $1.8 million, you would have to show that the business is capable of producing profits of $600,000 a year.

You also might be overvaluing your business because of inaccurate financial numbers. That's what happened to one of my eeCPA clients who had comingled funds without disclosing it to us. This client was a cannabis business run by two brothers where one brother was planning to sell his share in the business to the other brother, who was then going to invite an outside investor to come in and make a $25 million investment into the business.

During the due diligence process, three different sets of professionals reviewed the accounts. They did historical reviews validating the previous year's financials and the current year's financials. During this process they even requested legal documents from three or four years ago. We at eeCPA were responsible for having all this information readily available. We tried to make the accounts look as good as possible, but this particular enterprise was still in its early stages and was not quite producing a profit yet.

A major issue came to light during this process. The brother who wanted to sell his share kept saying, "The business owes me $11 million," but according to the books we had, the business owed him only $7 million. It turned out that he had been using personal accounts and accounts from his other businesses to cover the cannabis business's expenses. Whenever a bill came in and the business didn't have money to cover it, he would take whatever checkbook he had money in and write a check out of that account. So he had been writing checks for the cannabis business's expenses, such as legal and consulting fees, from all these different LLCs and personal accounts. We at eeCPA had no way of knowing, because we weren't managing any of these other accounts and never received any of the bills in question.

Once we found this out, we were able to go back and record all the expenses properly, thus increasing the loan the business owed him by $4 million, from $7 million to $11 million. Unfortunately, this also created a $4 million loss in the company's books. We'd started this process with what was already a bit of a loss, but we'd been able to still show the buyer positive forecasts. Once this additional $4 million debt was uncovered, the outside investor got cold feet and walked away from the whole deal. Because of massive comingling of funds and bad bookkeeping, they lost out on a potential $25 million investment.

Comingling of funds is incredibly common with entrepreneurs who are involved in multiple business enterprises. They look at all their ventures as one big business, and so they take cash from wherever it is available and don't go back to adjust the books accordingly. This approach can cause major problems later on down the line, as it did for this cannabis client. The simplest way to avoid this issue is simply to transfer money to the correct business that is incurring the expense and then pay that expense out of the appropriate business account.

If the cannabis company hadn't comingled funds, we

would have been working from the proper numbers up front, and we could have come up with a different story, a new financial model that would have worked. To make that story work, we likely would have needed to hold off on the sale for a year or two, so that the brothers could make some changes to show the business in a better light, but then the $25 million investment would have gone through.

The business is in trouble now. The $25 million investment was supposed to repay the one brother the $11 million he'd invested, pay the other brother $7 million that he was due, and put $7 million toward fixing their cultivation operation. Now, in addition to the business being in trouble, the family is fighting too. They're not going to be able to get outside investment in the current state the business is in, so they're going to have to make some changes. They might even have to go backward a step to chapter 4 and form a debt-management plan.

PROCESS FOR SELLING A BUSINESS

So you want to sell your business. Maybe you're burned out or can't get ahead, or maybe you just want to retire or pursue new ventures. Whatever the case, the process will largely be the same.

You can list the business with a broker or privately, and after that, there are three steps to the sale:

1. Verbal agreement
2. Terms sheet
3. Due diligence

In the verbal agreement stage, you and the buyer negotiate a purchase price for the business. Then the terms sheet lays out the specifics of the sale. After that comes the due diligence period, which typically lasts at least three to four weeks. Due diligence is when the business's accounting system comes to light. During this time the buyer will go through all your financial statements, tax returns, and bank statements and try to independently verify or audit your books to make sure that what you say you're selling them is what they're actually receiving. Sales can easily fall through during due diligence, so you want to prepare ahead of time.

HOW TO PREPARE FOR A SALE

To get the best price for your business, you want to have a lot of cash, low debt, high profit, and a good, clean accounting system in place. There are several different steps you can take to help get those key factors in place and prepare for the sale of your business.

PLAN AHEAD

You need to give yourself a long lead time to get the best possible price. Don't put yourself into a fire-sale situation where you have to take the first offer. If you're in a position where a fire sale is your only option, it is what it is, but these sales usually don't turn out well. If you have any choice in the matter, plan a lead time of at least a year or two. In this time, there's a lot you can do to present your business in the best light: you can make aggressive tax moves, implement upgrades, clean up your accounting system, and do some financial forecasting.

Part of planning ahead is considering the tax implications of the sale. Let's say you expect to get $1 million for the sale of your business. Of the $1 million you receive, how much of it do you get to keep? Many entrepreneurs have an exit strategy but don't bring in a tax expert, and then they're surprised by how much tax they get hit with following the sale.

The amount of tax you owe will differ depending on how your business is structured, so you definitely want to get a tax evaluation. If you plan ahead enough, you can potentially restructure to reduce your owed taxes on the sale. There are a variety of other strategies that can mitigate the tax impact too, but some of them are very complicated. Because there are so many different strategies possible and because the right plan will depend on your specific business, it is best to consult an expert for strategy.

MAKE AGGRESSIVE TAX MOVES

If you want to sell your business and get top dollar, you're going to have to make a paradigm shift in how you think about taxes. For the life of your business, you've probably been focused on saving money on taxes. One common tax-saving strategy is to take on big expenses to lower your tax bill. However, it is hard to prove that such expenses were made as a tax move. To a buyer, they just look like big expenses that have resulted in lower profit. So instead, now you might have to pay more taxes in order to show more profits and thus get a better price on the sale.

If you consult a tax expert, there are other, more complicated tax moves you can make too. For instance, in 2016, I had a family who sold a building (which they had originally purchased on a note in 2009 for $14.2 million) for about $30 million. This family had been clients of eeCPA for years, and thus we were engaged for tax strategy in conjunction with the sale.

We took a three-pronged approach to save them as much money as possible: we (1) gifted interests in the real estate LLC to the founding couple's children, (2) split the parcel and did a 1031 exchange, and (3) recommended an installment sale.

The first step is a strategy that should ideally be employed years before the sale commences. Plan ahead! In this case, starting two years before the sale in 2014, we began gifting interests in the building to the client's children. In addition to gifting the interests (at substantial discounts to reduce potential estate tax liability), we had the couple employ their children to manage the building. The children then reinvested all the money they earned to purchase additional units in the real estate LLC that owned the building. The client was in the 37% tax bracket, while the children were in the 15% tax bracket, resulting in significant savings of 22% plus on the ordinary rental income generated from the lease on the building.

Next, we did something ingenious, if I do say so myself. I honestly still can't believe I thought of doing this. While looking up the property in county records, I discovered that even though it was a single building with a parking lot, it was technically *two* parcels. So instead of selling it in a single transaction, I negotiated with the buyer to split it into two sales, one for each parcel—one parcel for $10 million and one parcel for $20 million.

We were then able to defer all the tax on the $10 million sale by putting it into a 1031 exchange (which is a benefit under Internal Revenue Code 1031 where an investor can defer all capital gains tax on the sale of a property if they reinvest all the proceeds into a new property or properties). By splitting the building into two parcels and then investing the proceeds from one of the parcels into new pieces of property, the couple was able to avoid the approximately 28% tax (20% federal capital gains tax, plus 3.8% net investment income tax, plus 4.5% Arizona state tax) on the $10 million, meaning a savings of $2.8 million. Had we not split the parcels, the couple would have been forced to acquire replacement property worth $30 million in order to qualify under the 1031 exchange rules. It would have been very difficult for them to do that without acquiring more debt, which they did not wish to do. The $10 million reinvestment, on the other hand, was in line with their goals.

Finally, the last part of our strategy was to do an installment sale on the $20 million parcel. We spread the sale out over two years, with the client receiving $17 million in 2016 and then $3 million in 2017. This way, the client had to pay taxes on only the $17 million in 2016. The client had been making payments on the $14.2 million note, but they still had about $14 million in debt. The $17 million was enough to pay back this debt as well as the taxes. The client was then able to postpone the tax on the remaining $3 million, received in 2017, until April 2018. With this strategy, the client wasn't necessarily *saving* tax, but we were able to defer their tax to give them use of the cash for another twelve months.

ONLY MAKE PURCHASES THAT IMPACT ROI

If you plan to sell your business soon, consider only purchases that will impact your ROI.

If you're selling your house, upgrading your kitchen or bathroom will get you more money, but upgrading your garage probably won't do anything for you. Potential buyers may not care about a garage, but everyone cares about kitchens and bathrooms.

You should adopt the same logic with the sale of your business. Only make purchases that are going to absolutely make your business better. This isn't a time to invest in testing new marketing or sales strategies that may not pan out. Focus on making the most profit that you can at this point.

CLEAN UP YOUR ACCOUNTING SYSTEM

To get the best price, you want to have a good financial statement to offer the buyer. That statement needs to be supported by a rock-solid accounting system, because your buyer is going to send someone to nitpick your books. A whole team of professionals will come in and compare your financial statements against bank statements and other source documents to make sure that the numbers are accurate and that what you're promising is what the buyer is actually getting. If there are mistakes, they will come to light, and not only can these impact the selling price negatively, but they can also make the buyer lose faith in you.

The best way to prepare for the due diligence phase is to clean up your accounting system in advance. I recommend bringing in a professional. This way, you have an expert who can not only ensure the information is accurate but also defend the accounting system for you.

As you work on cleaning up your books, you want to be heavy in cash and low in debt, and you want to have an impressive profit and loss statement. If any of those pieces is missing, you need to take action to help improve those numbers before the sale. You also want to keep an eye out for comingling of funds, as this is a huge cause of inaccurate numbers, as in the case of the cannabis business owned by two brothers. Also, be sure that the information is current, with all invoices and bills recorded into the system. You might have $1 million in revenue, but if you've recorded only $500,000 worth of invoices, that's what the buyer will consider the true revenue.

Be careful about giving out interim financial statements.

Big expenses can show up as losses on interim statements if they're not listed as accrued expenses. Say, for example, that you don't use the accrual method for accounting and you pay $18,000 every March for software for the next twelve months. If you give a buyer your financial statements from January through March, that $18,000 software expense will show up as a huge loss for you in March. In reality, only one-twelfth of that amount, or $1,500, is an actual expense for that month, as the remaining eleven-twelfths pays for software for the next eleven months. But all a buyer is going to see is that you're making much less profit in March than expected.

DO SOME FORECASTING

Skilled forecasting can make a huge difference in the sale of your business. A lot of business owners focus only on customer contracts and facilities when they're trying to sell their business. Those things are certainly important—good, long-term contracts with customers; clean, well-operated facilities; and professional, committed employees are definitely attractive to buyers.

But buyers will look at you from all directions, not just customer contracts and facilities. When a buyer walks in the door, you want to show them how they can make money from your business. This will put you in a better position to get a good price.

Some people can't visualize what something looks like when it's completed, though. In real estate, for example, people can't visualize what a house will look like with furniture in it. This is why many houses, especially high-end ones, will be staged with all the bells and whistles—to paint a picture for potential buyers. When potential buyers walk into a staged home, they fall in love with it, immediately able to picture themselves living there.

Imagine you're staging your business for the sale, just like you'd stage a home. For you to get the best price, the buyer needs to be able to see a story, a vision. Why should they acquire your business? What are they going to get out of it? Show them how they can make a huge profit from your business. If they can picture themselves owning the business and making money, they'll be more open to your desired price. Whatever price you want for your business, you need to show the buyer how they can get that money back and make a return on their investment within at least three years.

This story starts with the financial statements and the yearly profits the business has already shown. That's just the baseline, though—the minimum expected profit. Show the buyer all the ways they could increase that profit. The best way to do this is to create various financial models for the buyer. Show them how much the profit would increase if they increased sales at x rate throughout the year or cut certain expenses. For example, maybe you're taking a $250,000 salary. You could show the buyer that by hiring a manager for $125,000 instead, they'd get $125,000 more profit each year. Because a business's value is often priced at three times the yearly profit, that financial modeling could add $375,000 to your asking price.

Your financials will form the basis for the sale, but having that story to show potential investors what is in it for them if they buy your business is like icing on the cake and can help seal the deal.

WHAT CAN HAPPEN IF YOU DON'T PREPARE—A CAUTIONARY TALE

You want to take all these steps to prepare your business for sale not only to prevent your price being cut during due diligence but also to make sure you're properly valuing your business. While many business owners tend to think their business is worth more than it is, like Jim from the beginning of the chapter or the two brothers with their marijuana business, other business owners undervalue their business. That's what happened with Tom.

Tom hired eeCPA to do just the tax strategy portion for the sale of his waste management business. He had ongoing problems with getting a qualified bookkeeper and office manager, so his books were very messy. He cleaned things up enough to make the sale to a regional operator, one of the big waste management companies in the area.

After the sale was made, the buyer transferred all of Tom's clients into their own billing and accounting system. Soon, they discovered that Tom had been underbilling his clients by $30,000 a month. So the buyer got a 15% increase in the bottom line right off the bat—$360,000 more profit per year than expected.

Had Tom reviewed his books better and realized how much more profit his business could have been making, he may not have sold it at all. Or if he had decided to still sell it, he could have gotten a much higher price. Factoring in the extra $360,000 yearly profit over the first three years, Tom could have asked for at least an extra $1 million.

I cannot stress enough how expensive accounting mistakes can be. If Tom had a better system in place and a decent bookkeeper, he could have caught this underbilling issue much sooner. Up until the sale, all that underbilling was money taken directly out of Tom's pocket. If eeCPA had been in charge of more than just the tax strategy, I believe we would have caught this discrepancy and would have been able to propose and support a higher price with the proper forecasting.

BUYING A BUSINESS

When you're buying a business, your goal is to uncover any potential issues in the business before you purchase it. You absolutely must hire a consultant to review the business for you in the due diligence phase. The consultant will prevent you from making a bad investment and can unearth issues that could result in huge discounts for you.

I had one client who had set terms to purchase a medical spa for $395,000. In the due diligence phase, we discovered a lot of issues. Their books were messy, so they couldn't prove all their sources of revenue. For example, they had sales recorded in their point-of-sale system, but the resulting cash was never actually deposited in the company bank account. Because of all the issues we uncovered, we managed to get the seller to drop their price to $125,000.

In another instance, I had a client who was under contract to buy two Verizon stores for $450,000. In due diligence, when we matched the stores' financial statements against third-party source documents, such as bank statements, merchant statements, and corporate Verizon statements, we discovered that the numbers on the stores' financial statements were inaccurate. As a result, our client ended up getting about a 50% discount, acquiring both stores for just $225,000. These are significant discounts over what the seller could have gotten had they had a good accounting system and followed it.

As a buyer, the due diligence phase is absolutely critical. In many cases, hiring an experienced consultant will save you far more money than it costs. For instance, with the Verizon stores, that client paid us $22,000 and saved $225,000 as a result—that's nearly a 1,000% ROI!

FURTHER INFORMATION

- For more information about how to calculate your business's cash, see chapter 7, "Reconciling Your Accounts."
- For more on assets, see chapter 8, "Taking Inventory."
- For more on the accounting principles related to expenses, see chapter 12, "Breaking Even"; chapter 13, "Employing Folks"; and chapter 14, "Running the Business."

PART II

Good Accounting Practices

The first part of the book outlined what is at stake, showing how accounting mistakes can destroy your business and upend your life. Now it's time to make sure you don't become another cautionary tale. The second part of the book takes you through the nitty-gritty accounting practices that will ensure you and your business succeed.

The ensuing chapters will focus on the two financial documents most important to your business: the balance sheet and the profit and loss statement. Chapter 6 provides an introduction to these documents, and the subsequent chapters dive into detail on the major components of each document.

CHAPTER 6

MANAGING THE NUMBERS

THE BALANCE SHEET—THE IMPORTANCE OF NET WORTH

Accounting can be complex, but it doesn't need to be. There are two primary financial documents you need to concern yourself with: the balance sheet and the profit and loss (P&L) statement. The balance sheet is a snapshot of your business's financial status at a particular point in time, showing the business's assets, liabilities, and equity. The P&L shows the business's income and expenses over a designated period.

If you were to walk into my office as a client, you might think I'd first ask to see your P&L. Wrong! Most business owners think it's most important to focus on the business's income and expenses, because these are the things that indicate whether a business is profitable. However, the health of the business is actually determined by its net worth, which is what the balance sheet shows.

To understand the importance of net worth, think about your personal bank account. Let's say you make $200,000 a year. After deducting all your living expenses, you manage to put away $20,000 in savings. If you had a personal P&L, you'd show a net income of $20,000. Not too bad. But let's say that $20,000 is all you have saved in your bank account, and you also have a $250,000 mortgage, a $50,000 car loan, and $50,000 of credit card debt. The house is valued at $275,000, while the car is valued at $25,000 according to Kelley Blue Book. So, total, you have $350,000 of debt and only $320,000 of assets. While your P&L shows a fairly positive picture, your balance sheet would reveal that, in reality, you're underwater, with a net worth of -$30,000. If you suddenly lost your job, how long would you be able to survive?

Net Worth Table

Assets

Cash	20,000
Car	25,000
Primary Residence	275,000
Total Assets	320,000

Liabilities

Credit Card Debt	50,000
Car Loan	50,000
Mortgage	250,000
Total Liabilities	350,000
Net Worth	(30,000)

As a business, you need to know your net worth, and you want it to be a positive number. Knowing your business's net worth allows you to make strategic decisions on how to use your resources, and when you have a positive net worth, you are better able to withstand potential setbacks in the future. For example, what if you lose a major customer? What if there's a downturn in the economy? What if a key employee gets sick?

Many business owners will take constant draws off their business to support their lifestyle, regardless of whether the business is making a profit or not. This can quickly push a business into a negative net worth, which is a dangerous place to be. You could back yourself into a corner where you're unable to cover your fixed operating costs and have to close your doors.

So if you came into my office, I would first ask to see your balance sheet so that I could get a snapshot of your overall financial health. I would take you through the parts of the balance sheet and show you what areas you should be thinking about and why thinking about these pieces is critical to your business. After that, we'd go through the elements of the P&L.

PARTS OF THE BALANCE SHEET

The balance sheet has four parts: cash, assets, liabilities, and equity.

CASH

One of the first questions I ask new clients is how much cash their business has, as cash is a key component to whether a business will be able to survive a setback. A business's cash is all their current assets that are liquid.

Chapter 7, "Reconciling Your Accounts," details how to accurately tally your cash reserves and discusses how much of a cash reserve you need to keep your business afloat in case of a rough patch or downturn.

ASSETS

There are three types of assets: current assets, long-term fixed assets, and intangible assets.

Besides cash, current assets include anything that you can reasonably expect to convert to cash within a year, such as inventory and accounts receivable.

Long-term fixed assets are all your assets that can't easily be converted into cash, such as computer equipment, vehicles, and real estate. These things can be liquidated; it just takes time.

Intangible assets are things that may not have a clear cash value, such as intellectual property or goodwill.

Chapter 8, "Taking Inventory," discusses how to manage and track your assets and offers tips on making sure you actually collect on your accounts receivable.

LIABILITIES

Liabilities are broken down into current liabilities and long-term liabilities. Current liabilities reflect debt that must be paid off in the next year, unless you renegotiate the terms of the debt, and long-term liabilities are those debts not due within the current year.

If you have a long-term loan, the payments due in the next year are considered current liabilities, while the remaining payments are classified as long-term liabilities. Let's say you borrow $1 million on a twenty-year mortgage. You're going to be paying roughly $50,000 a year in principal payments on that debt. So your current liability would be $50,000, and your long-term liability would be $950,000.

Chapter 9, "Cutting Your Losses," discusses all the various current and long-term liabilities your business might face, including liabilities you may currently be overlooking.

EQUITY

Equity is all the money invested into a business from non-lending institutions (e.g., money you personally put into your business or money that shareholders invest) and all the accumulated and retained earnings of the business, including current profit.

Chapter 10, "Building Equity," looks at the components of equity and the impact different types of entity structures can have on equity.

P&L STATEMENT

The P&L represents the current activities of your business. At its core, it answers the question, "Are you operating at a profit or a loss?"

The P&L helps you think about making and spending money, as it shows you all the various income and expenses of your business.

Many times, you will use the P&L to figure out how to maximize profit. You will look for places where you can cut expenses and increase income.

In other cases, depending on your long-term vision for your business, it might make sense for you to be operating at a loss or on a tight margin. Especially in a growing business, you may reinvest the majority of your profits back into the business in order to drive future revenue. For example, you may hire new employees in anticipation of a higher volume of business coming down the pipeline.

In this case, you will use the P&L to make sure that the expenses are resulting in an increase in top-line revenue that will eventually result in a profit to cover the expenses. If your P&L shows that you're operating at a loss and revenue isn't increasing, then what you're doing isn't working, and you need to make a change.

Whatever your goal with your business, the P&L will be key to helping you make your decisions.

PARTS OF THE P&L

The main parts of the P&L statement are revenue, direct costs, labor costs, and general and administrative costs and occupancy costs.

REVENUE

Revenue is all the money coming into your business. When revenue exceeds expenses, you are operating at a profit.

Chapter 11, "Getting Paid," covers the best practices for tracking revenue and discusses how to properly categorize revenue in alignment with direct costs.

DIRECT COSTS

Direct costs are all the costs needed to support the customer, or the costs needed to produce revenue.

Sometimes sales and marketing costs are direct costs, such as when salespeople are paid a commission. Other times, these costs are indirect. On your P&L, you will record the direct sales and marketing costs under direct costs, and you will create a separate category for the remaining sales and marketing costs.

Chapter 12, "Breaking Even," discusses direct costs, including how to determine when costs such as sales and marketing are direct costs and when they belong in another bucket of expenses.

LABOR COSTS

Labor costs are all the costs associated with employing people, not just the salaries you pay them. For example, labor costs also include payroll taxes, payroll processing fees, employee benefits and bonuses, recruiting costs, team building or culture exercises, and employee expense reimbursements (for example, travel mileage or incidentals).

Chapter 13, "Employing Folks," looks at the various costs of employing people and discusses how to make hiring decisions, including the pros and cons of outsourcing professional services.

GENERAL AND ADMINISTRATIVE COSTS AND OCCUPANCY COSTS

General and administrative costs and occupancy costs are your overhead—the costs that are needed to keep the business running but aren't direct costs.

General and administrative costs include things such as insurance, office supplies, and licensing fees. These costs tend to be small, but they can add up quickly.

These costs also include computer and software costs (excluding the costs of physical hardware)—for example, cybersecurity, software, apps, point-of-sale systems, and so on. If these costs are significant for your company, then it's best to pull them out into their own category separate from the rest of the general and administrative costs.

Occupancy costs include things such as rent, facilities costs (the cost to maintain the facilities), property taxes, and utilities.

Chapter 14, "Running the Business," looks at how to track and audit these various small expenses to identify savings opportunities. It also discusses the various factors you should take into consideration when deciding on a business space, including whether to buy or rent.

THE PURPOSE OF THE BALANCE SHEET AND THE P&L

Your balance sheet and P&L are the keys to assessing the health and profitability of your business. They are intended to be big-picture sources of information. They can alert you to potential issues and point you in the right direction.

While the balance sheet and P&L are absolutely critical, they are just one source of information. If something seems off on either your balance sheet or P&L, you'll want to drill down into more detail to more specifically identify and then solve the issue.

In addition, on a daily and weekly basis, you will need to rely on other reports and numbers, as the balance sheet and P&L are designed to be monthly financial statements, not weekly or daily. As well as monitoring your financial statements, you should also keep track of key performance indicators, such as number of sales, customer satisfaction, number of prospects in the pipeline, and so on.

Even though your balance sheet and P&L aren't the only reports you will need to be successful, they are the foundation on which you will build your business.

CHAPTER 7

RECONCILING YOUR ACCOUNTS

DO YOU HAVE AS MUCH CASH AS YOU THINK YOU DO?

Whenever I get a new client, I always start with the cash section of the balance sheet. I'm interested in two main questions: "How much cash do you have?" and "How many accounts do you have?" To answer these questions, we tally up all the sources of cash and list them out by account on the balance sheet.

Here's an example of what this section of the balance sheet might look like for a service company. (For a full copy of this example balance sheet, see the appendix.)

Excerpt Cash

	12/31/17	12/31/16	Change
Cash			
Chase Checking 3906	13,295	44,661	(31,366)
Chase Money Market 4244	6,011	55,041	(49,030)
Petty Cash	40	495	(455)
Gift Cards	1,140	1,440	(300)
Total Cash	**20,486**	**101,637**	**(81,151)**

TYPES OF CASH

Your business's cash includes all the current assets that you can liquidate essentially immediately. Aside from the cash you have in your various business checking and savings accounts, the following are the main types of cash you'll likely have:

- Petty cash—the cash you have on hand to buy pizza for your employees, purchase emergency supplies from Staples, and so on.
- Retail tills—the cash you keep in your registers to tender transactions.
- Cash in a safe—the cash you keep on premises in a safe (for cash-intensive business).
- Undeposited funds—payments received from customers that have not been deposited to your business bank account yet, such as undeposited checks. This

category basically represents deposits in transit. It is helpful to list these funds separately from the other cash assets because they have not been fully negotiated yet and are not available for spending.

- Pending deposits—the cash you have deposited into an account that hasn't actually shown up yet. When you deposit a check, you might not have access to the funds right away if the bank believes the check may not clear. Maybe you've overdrawn your account in the past, or maybe you just recently started your business and don't yet have a record of longevity at your bank. In these cases, your bank won't deposit the funds into your account until the check clears.
- Bank card transactions—the cash from pending merchant transactions. If you swipe a customer's card today, the money will be in limbo for a couple of days before actually making it into your bank account.

COMMON MISCONCEPTIONS ABOUT CASH

MYTH #1: YOUR BANK ACCOUNT BALANCE IS YOUR CASH TOTAL

With online banking, everyone can quickly log into their bank account and immediately check their balance. An online balance doesn't tell the whole story, though, so you can't simply check your balance and assume that is the amount of cash you have. If you do that, you're not taking into account any pending transactions, whether it's pending deposits or pending payables.

I previously mentioned a client of mine who will cut checks but then wait to mail them out until he gets enough money into his account. If he checks his online bank account balance, it might tell him he has $60,000. If he checks his accounting system, though, he actually has –$60,000. If he was relying on only the number he saw online, he could mistakenly spend money that he doesn't really have.

It's also easy to forget about automatic debits that are scheduled to take place. For example, you might autopay your utility bill each month. Autopay is an excellent way to ensure your bills are paid on time while giving you one less thing to think about. If you glance at your bank account balance and forget about a pending debit, though, you will have a false idea of how much money you have.

For example, let's say your monthly utility bill is $10,000, due on the twelfth of each month. You look at your account on the eleventh, see you have $12,000, and write out $5,000 worth of checks, thinking you have plenty of money to cover them. Then, on the twelfth, $10,000 is deducted for your utility bill, leaving you with only $2,000 in the account—not enough to cover the $5,000 in checks you've already sent out. Hopefully, you have a reserve in a savings account to back up your checking account, so you aren't bouncing checks, but you're still going to be overdrawing the account and racking up fees fast.

Instead of relying on online account balances, track your cash in your accounting system. This way, you can make all the necessary subtractions and additions of pending transactions to calculate your true cash total.

MYTH #2: HAVING MORE ACCOUNTS IS BETTER

Many people believe it's best to have a separate dedicated bank account for each aspect of the business—for example, an account for all sales and marketing expenses, an account for all rent expenses, and so on. I strongly disagree with this philosophy. Two bank accounts—one checking account and one savings account—is plenty for most businesses.

First and foremost, having dozens of different accounts is unnecessarily complex. Frankly, the more accounts you have, the more likely you are to get confused and make mistakes. You will constantly have to keep track of which account you're supposed to be using. Which account do the utilities come out of? What about software? Liability insurance? Maybe you have a bill you need to pay immediately, but you don't have the funds in the right account. Now you have to rush and transfer money to the needed account before paying the bill or risk comingling funds. Once you start comingling the funds—using the operating account to cover payroll or pulling from the marketing account to cover travel expenses—the balances are no longer as meaningful, and you've essentially ruined the whole system.

The rationale behind having multiple accounts is to keep track of expenses in the different cost buckets, but if you have a good accounting system, it will already do that for you. And you won't have to worry about accidentally comingling funds and throwing off all the data.

In addition, you have your own threshold of tolerance for the minimum you need in your account before getting nervous. With multiple accounts, you have that many more minimums to keep track of. Plus, totaled together, you may need to keep more money in reserve. If you had just one checking account, maybe you'd be fine with a $20,000 minimum. If you have six different accounts, though, maybe you'd want minimums of $1,000, $5,000, $10,000, $3,000, $4,000, and $7,000, because each category needs its own buffer. That's an extra $10,000 you need to hold in reserve. In any case, the fewer accounts you have, the simpler it is to manage. Plus, you will save money on fees and accounting.

When you have multiple bank accounts, you are also opening yourself up to that many more opportunities for fraud.

I recently chatted with a C-suite executive with a very prominent real estate development company that builds apartment communities throughout the Phoenix valley and other areas of the country. They discovered that fraud had taken place, so they went to the state attorney general and hired a well-regarded, top-ten national CPA firm to determine the source and extent of the fraud. The firm was able to identify the CFO as the source, but after billing the client more than $1.5 million in accounting fees, the firm still couldn't issue a report to assess exactly how much the CFO had stolen over time, although they estimated it was at least $7.5 million.

The reason they couldn't assess the full damage was the CFO had created *seventy* different bank accounts for the business—one for each property—all in the name of "organization." In reality, he used the accounts to constantly move money back and forth, skimming a little off the top each time. He didn't always update the books to reflect these transactions, so with the constant transfers, the money became impossible to track.

The risk of having multiple accounts open—from an embezzlement standpoint and an accuracy standpoint—

far outweighs the benefits. Unless you're bringing in millions of dollars of revenue, keep it simple and have one checking account and one savings account.

MYTH #3: A SEPARATE PAYROLL ACCOUNT IS A NECESSITY

You don't need a separate payroll account. You can have your payroll paid from your operating account, and a proper accounting system will record all the needed information.

However, if you *want* to have a separate account for your payroll, you can definitely do that. A separate payroll account is typically the only additional account I tell my clients is OK to have. You *need* only a checking account and a savings account, but having a third payroll account won't complicate things too much.

BEST PRACTICES: HOW TO BETTER MANAGE YOUR CASH

LIMIT THE NUMBER OF ACCOUNTS

Again, less is more. Fewer accounts mean fewer moving parts and fewer things to manage. Have a savings account, which will function as your reserve account, a checking account, and potentially a payroll account.

Simple is better. Reduce complexity where you can, and make your life easier!

ENTER EVERYTHING

Keep track of all the kinds of cash your business has, not just your bank account balances. Also, be sure to record automatic debits. Don't rely on your memory or online banking. You never know when you'll forget something—better safe than sorry.

Also, when possible, I recommend limiting automatic debits. Sometimes various vendors and other organizations aren't consistent on when they process automatic debits. Maybe they say they will do it the fifteenth of each month, but then one month they don't sweep the funds until the twentieth or, worse, they process them early, on the tenth. Such timing discrepancies could easily cause issues for you.

Also, many bills can vary tremendously, such as utility bills. Whether it is winter in the northeast or summer in the southwest, your utility bill could easily triple depending on the season. If you're manually paying these bills instead of using autopay, there will be fewer surprises, and you can make sure you have enough in your account to cover the bill.

However, a lot of places offer discounts if you sign up for direct pay, and direct pay does make things easier. So if you do want to use direct pay, just be sure to do it with a credit card and not a debit card. That way, the autopay won't affect your amount of cash in the bank. You can also time your credit card statement cutoff date to occur right before the majority of your expenses are due. This can buy you an extra thirty days to make payments on those balances.

Make sure you account for all the credit card transactions and keep updated account balances of how much is on your credit card. With all the amazing technology we have today, you can link your credit card transactions directly into your accounting system to keep an up-to-the-minute pulse on your credit card activity.

RECONCILE REGULARLY

It is important to regularly reconcile your accounts. Make sure the information you see in your online bank balance matches up with what your accounting system says you have, taking into account any pending transactions, whether they're undeposited checks, pending deposits, bank card transactions, or upcoming debits.

HAVE CASH RESERVES AND A LINE OF CREDIT AS A BUFFER

I recommend keeping both a buffer of cash and a line of credit.

For a service company, set aside a minimum cash reserve of one month of payroll. For a retail company, set aside at least one month of payroll plus one month of average purchases and labor costs you anticipate outside of employees on your payroll. You need to factor in these two additional categories for a retail business because you rely on them to fulfill your sales.

This one-month guideline is the minimum. If you're operating with less than that, you will have fewer options and will have to spend more time to manage those funds carefully. Ideally, you'd actually have at least two months of payroll for a service company and two months of payroll and average purchases and labor costs for a retail company.

In calculating this minimum cash reserve, don't worry about including all the operating expenses of the business—the general and administrative costs of running the business, the software costs, the occupancy costs, and the sales and marketing costs. Focus on the cost of labor and materials. These will be the largest costs you have, and they are the costs that will drive your ability to fulfill your sales. The other costs are overhead and don't drive the business engine in the same way. If you can't pay for labor and materials, you can't make money and get yourself through whatever slump you're in, and then you have a major problem.

In addition to your one-month cash reserve, if your business qualifies, get a line of credit that can cover an additional two months' worth of direct costs. If you're a service company with a monthly payroll of $50,000, for example, try to get a $100,000 line of credit.

Having a line of credit allows you to bid on larger-value contracts that may take longer to pay out. Sometimes you may need to pay for labor and materials expenses for a job before getting paid by the customer. If you don't have a line of credit, then you may have to borrow from other sources to cover the expenses. You may even have to use a credit card, and it is always a bad idea to finance things on a credit card because the interest rates are so high. Or you may have to turn the job down entirely because you can't sustain your business while you wait to get paid.

A line of credit can also help you stay afloat in case of an emergency, such as the loss of a large customer or a lawsuit, and can also be used to help you grow and expand. For example, it could provide the funding needed to open another service offering, create a new product, or hire new people and purchase additional equipment in order to fulfill a sizable new contract.

A line of credit is useful because, for many businesses, especially startups, it's simply not feasible to save up this amount of money in cash. When you draw from your line of credit, you should work to quickly repay the debt.

With a cash reserve and line of credit, you will be able to weather setbacks and take advantage of opportunities.

MAKE A CASH-FLOW FORECAST

Besides having the absolute minimum reserves on hand, it is critical that at any given time you have a ninety-day cash-flow forecast. You should know how much cash you have available, what your liabilities are, what money you expect to come in from customers in the next ninety days, and what needs to be paid in the coming ninety days. With this forecast, you can identify and plan for any potential hiccups.

Here's an example of what a ninety-day cash-flow forecast might look like:

MedSpa Cash Flow Tool (2018)

	Activity	Actual					Forecast		
		January	February	March	April	May	June	July
Beginning Cash Balance		6,170	7,435	45,270	75	7,810	21,360	17,910
		Inflows						
Sales	Operating	46,969	45,269	68,858	55,475	60,000	62,000	64,000
Total Income		**46,969**	**45,269**	**68,858**	**55,475**	**60,000**	**62,000**	**64,000**
		Outflows						
Cost of Goods Sold	Operating	5,429	21,124	15,560	14,427	21,000	21,700	22,400
G&A	Operating	10,286	8,716	12,196	10,056	9,000	10,000	9,000
Sales and Marketing	Operating	1,028	1,316	630	1,025	750	950	1,100
Occupancy Costs	Operating	6,383	6,367	6,403	6,448	6,400	6,400	6,400
Staffing Costs	Operating	17,364	23,277	32,251	20,438	21,000	21,000	21,000
Other Expenses	Operating	1,211	720	797	949	800	800	800
Total Expenses		**41,702**	**61,520**	**67,837**	**53,343**	**58,950**	**60,850**	**60,700**
Net Operating Income		**5,268**	**(16,251)**	**1,021**	**2,132**	**1,050**	**1,150**	**3,300**

continued…

172 · PROTECT YOUR PROFIT

		Adjustments						
Undeposited Funds	Operating	(571)	3,914	(4,100)	7,130	(1,000)	(1,000)	(1,000)
Inventory (Purchases)/Sales	Operating					(15,000)	7,500	7,500
Credit Card Charges/(Payments)	Operating	(2,128)	(39,743)	1,673	(1,770)	(2,000)	(2,000)	(2,000)
Gift Certificates Sold/(Redeemed)	Operating	1,488	(2,698)	(2,082)	(1,251)	(1,500)	(1,500)	3,000
Payroll Liabilities	Operating	(368)	195	2,936	(170)	-		
Sales Tax Payable	Operating	26	(193)	67	(29)	-		
Depreciation & Amortization	Investing	800	800	800	800	800	800	800
Line of Credit Advances	Financing		99,600	-	9,292	40,000	-	
Loan Payments	Financing	(3,250)	(7,789)	(45,511)	(8,400)	(8,800)	(8,400)	(8,800)
Total Adjustments		**(4,003)**	**54,086**	**(46,217)**	**5,603**	**12,500**	**(4,600)**	**(500)**
Ending Cash Balance		**7,435**	**45,270**	**75**	**7,810**	**21,360**	**17,910**	**20,710**

If your forecast reveals that cash is going to be tight, take action immediately. If you're always chasing your tail, eking by at the last minute, then you will miss all the opportunities to proactively work your way through difficult periods when you have limited cash available to your business. You have many ways to mitigate low cash as long as you plan ahead.

To get through a low-cash period, you want to reduce and delay expenses while increasing incoming cash.

To reduce and delay expenses, work out favorable terms with vendors ahead of time. They will be much more likely to work with you if you contact them before you can't pay an invoice than if you wait until you're already in the red with them. If you're due to pay within thirty days of invoicing, perhaps you can stretch the due date out to forty-five or sixty days. Or you might be able to work out a payment plan, where you make weekly payments over the next ninety days.

To increase your cash flow, you can renegotiate with your customers, modify your sales contracts, offer discounts to people who pay in advance, and drive sales numbers.

Sometimes you need to think outside the box. For example, for the past fifteen years at eeCPA, we've typically charged customers for their tax returns once we complete the return. However, for some customers, the tax return process ends up taking quite a while because they don't have the records or we're waiting for corrected statements. We may start working on the return (and paying our team) in January, but we may not actually file the return until April. That's ninety days where we have to fund multiple expenses before bringing in any income.

This delay in payment usually wasn't an issue, but in 2017, I made a lot of investments into the business's growth, including a move to new facilities. These investments, coupled with the delay in payment, stretched our cash flow to a tighter margin than normal.

Because I regularly do ninety-day forecasts and always keep track of our cash reserves, I made the proactive decision to convert a significant majority of our clients to a monthly subscription at a discounted rate. Total, with the monthly plan, we don't get as much as with our one-time fees, but we're able to get money in January, February, and March instead of just in April. By getting the money in sooner, spread over time, we've normalized our cash flow throughout the year.

Instead of a subscription model of payment, you could also choose to link payments to milestones. In construction, for example, you often request a customer deposit of at least 50% for materials and then receive the remaining 50% at the end of the project, which might not be for another six months. To normalize your cash flow, instead of taking a 50% deposit, you could redo your contracts to set up certain milestones that trigger a payment installment from the customer.

At some point, your business will likely be short on cash. Whether the shortage is due to an unexpected setback, a regularly slow season, or investments to scale up, the extent to which you take proactive action will be the deciding factor in whether your business survives or fails.

KEY TIPS

- **Track how much cash you have available and create cash-flow forecasts.** When it comes to cash, the most important thing is to know how much you *really* have available right now and in the next ninety days. Is the cash you have already obligated to an upcoming expense? If so, then it is not really available cash.
- **Have adequate cash reserves.** For a service company, have one month of payroll on hand in cash reserves; for a retail company, have one month of payroll plus one month of materials and outside-labor costs. Cutting it closer than this will cause stress and poor business decisions. If you're strapped for cash, you don't have any leverage. You may enter into

agreements you're not happy with, and you may be forced to accept less-favorable terms, which might prolong the cash shortage. If you can jump ahead of the issue, you will have more options.

CHAPTER 8

TAKING INVENTORY

WHAT ASSETS DO YOU HAVE?

With every new client, after looking at the business's cash, I take inventory of all their other assets—all current, fixed, and intangible assets.

Here is an example of what the noncash assets portion of your balance sheet might look like:

Excerpt Cannabis Assets

	12/31/17	12/31/16	Change
Accounts Receivable			
Accounts Receivable	18,000	-	18,000
Total Accounts Receivable	18,000	-	18,000
Other Current Assets			
Work in Process: Manufacturing Facility	90,379	104,610	(14,231)
Related Party Loan Receivable	27,674	-	27,674
3rd Party Inventory	76,538		76,538
Homegrown Inventory	19,061		19,061
Total Inventory: Branch 1	95,599	-	95,599
3rd Party Inventory	75,698		75,698
Homegrown Inventory	28,600		28,600
Total Inventory: Branch 2	104,298	-	104,298
3rd Party Inventory	72,843		72,843
Homegrown Inventory	106,336		106,336
Total Inventory: Branch 3	179,179	-	179,179
Inventory: Manufacturing Facility	624,771	476,084	148,687
Prepaid Expenses	185,724	62,657	123,067
Undeposited Funds	-	3,080	(3,080)
Total Other Current Assets	1,307,623	646,431	661,192
Total Current Assets*	**1,669,527**	**749,947**	**919,580**

continued...

Fixed Assets			
Vehicles	44,960	13,068	31,892
Corporate Office Furniture	87,961	-	87,961
Corporate Office Equipment	3,122		3,122
Manufacturing Facility Machinery & Equipment	344,836	194,157	150,679
Manufacturing Facility Security System	12,514		12,514
Store Fixtures & Equipment	199,610		199,610
Tenant Improvements	5,912,723	4,002,151	1,910,572
Accumulated Depreciation	(1,027,817)	(591,243)	(436,574)
Total Fixed Assets	**5,577,909**	**3,618,133**	**1,959,776**
Other Assets			
MMJ License: Branch 1	600,000		600,000
MMJ License: Branch 3	2,525,000		2,525,000
Security Deposit: Manufacturing Facility	114,000	114,000	-
Security Deposit: Corporate Office	4,214	-	4,214
Total Other Assets	**3,243,214**	**114,000**	**3,129,214**

*Total Current Assets includes Cash not shown here.

CURRENT ASSETS (OTHER THAN CASH)

Aside from cash, a business's current assets include inventory, accounts receivable, intercompany loans, advances to shareholders, and prepaid expenses.

INVENTORY

For most wholesale and retail distributors, there is just

one type of inventory: all the things you sell. However, if you make, manufacture, or grow any type of product, then there are two types of inventory you should account for: the traditional inventory and also work in process. All of the costs to manufacture (supplies plus labor and applied overhead) should be posted to your work-in-process account as costs are incurred. Then, once the units are produced, you should move them out of work in process and into the inventory account, because they are now finished goods—stocked and ready to sell! All the inventory *that you can sell* is an asset. If your inventory is outdated or obsolete and thus unsalable, then it is not an asset.

ACCOUNTS RECEIVABLE

Accounts receivable is the money your customers owe you for a provided service or product. The portion of your accounts receivable that you can reasonably expect to collect is an asset.

INTERCOMPANY LOANS

Many business owners have multiple businesses and end up making intercompany loans, moving money from one business to another to cover a cash shortage, allow for investment, or the like. It is important to keep track of all these intercompany loans and make sure funds aren't being comingled without documentation. Assuming the other company has the money to pay back the loan in the next year, the loan is a current asset.

ADVANCES TO SHAREHOLDERS

Often, a business doesn't have enough profit to distribute to shareholders, but shareholders may need money and thus take advances. For example, as the business owner, you may need to take an advance out of the business to cover your personal expenses. As long as those advances can be repaid, they are assets.

PREPAID EXPENSES

Prepaid expenses—for example, prepayment of rent, insurance, or consultants—are listed on your balance sheet as an asset. Once it comes time to recognize those expenses on your P&L, they are removed as an asset from the balance sheet and moved to the P&L as an expense.

As an example, let's say you're going to send your people to a conference in July, and you pay $3,000 for the conference fees in February. Until your people go and experience the conference, you're not going to expense those funds. Until then, that $3,000 will sit on your balance sheet as a prepaid expense asset.

Or if you paid rent three months in advance, that money would also be listed as an asset on your balance sheet. Then, when the first of the next month rolls around, one month's worth of that amount would be marked as an expense on your P&L and the remaining two months of prepayment would remain on the balance sheet as an asset.

A lot of prepaid expenses can't be readily converted to cash. Be sure to take note of all cancelation and refund policies so that you know how much money you can get back if you need to cancel.

FIXED ASSETS

Fixed assets are long-term, physical assets, such as equipment, vehicles, and buildings. Fixed assets are things that you intend to use for an extended period for your everyday business and that are unlikely to be quickly converted to cash.

INTANGIBLE ASSETS

Intangible assets are nonphysical assets that have a long-term use.

Long-term loans to others, where you're getting repaid over time, and other long-term business investments are examples of intangible assets.

Goodwill is also a type of intangible asset. If you purchase another business, you gain the value of that company's brand name, its customer base, its business experience, and any patents or proprietary technology it has. All of that falls under goodwill.

Investing in a new type of copyrighted work is also a form of intangible asset. If you invest in a new process for a product you're building, you may not be able to readily convert those dollars to cash, but that intellectual property is an asset, one that you could potentially sell to another company someday.

COMMON MISCONCEPTIONS ABOUT ASSETS
MYTH #1: ACCOUNTS RECEIVABLES WILL BE PAID

Basically, every potential client tells me, "I don't have a receivables problem." Then I dive in and find they have an awful lot of receivables over ninety days. Most business owners don't see this as a problem, because they assume that the accounts receivables will be paid eventually. However, the more time you let pass, the less likely you are to actually receive payment.

People don't like confrontation, so a lot of smaller businesses in particular don't have effective processes around collecting accounts receivable. Asking for money from a customer can be an uncomfortable conversation, but it's a necessary one. You need to have clear processes in place for when to follow up about payment (see the "Best Practices" section below for specific tips). Letting too much time go by sets the wrong expectations and tone with your customers. You're essentially telling them, "I'm making so much money that I can't be bothered to follow up with you. I obviously don't need your money." If you don't follow up with your customers and set up payment plans when necessary, the receivable may go stale, and you may never get paid.

Now more than ever, you absolutely must follow up on receivables because there's a trend of not paying back debt. Back in the day, for baby boomers, maintaining excellent credit was critical, so that they could buy houses and the like. With the younger generation, people quickly get in over their heads with debt, starting with student loans, and they tank their credit early on. Debt has become so commonplace that having it doesn't have the same stigma it did fifty years ago. As a result, people aren't as concerned with repaying debt. They think, *I don't have the money right now, so I just won't pay that.*

If you don't manage your receivables and you wait for 120 days or more before you start following up on late payments, your ability to collect will be minimal. People will come up with any number of reasons why they won't pay their bills, including complaining about the quality of the service or the product they've already received and benefited from. To get the money you're owed, you might have to hire an attorney and go to court. It is much easier to simply stay on top of your receivables.

If you only made a sale on paper and never get the cash in hand, then you didn't really make the sale. But you still have to pay for all the expenses of that sale—paying your employees' wages, paying your supplier for a product that the customer isn't paying you for, and so on. Quickly, you may find yourself in an upside-down profit position.

MYTH #2: ALL INVENTORY HAS VALUE

Inventory is only worth what people are willing to pay for it. With time, inventory can go bad or become outdated, and it loses its value accordingly.

I had a client who owned a dressmaking shop who got a phenomenal price on a bunch of fabric. So she bought $600,000 worth. She thought she was getting a great deal, but she had too much fabric and couldn't sell it quickly enough. Because she wasn't making enough sales, she didn't have the money to make her scheduled payments on all this inventory, so she was losing about $35,000 a month in late fees and debt payments. Soon, the fabric went out of style, and she ended up having to sell it at a deep, deep discount. Her "great deal" ended up costing her much more than it saved.

With technology especially, products can quickly lose their value. Computer equipment is obsolete almost as soon as you install it. It seems like just yesterday that DVRs were invented, but they're already being phased out, replaced by Rokus and Apple TVs as television becomes more internet-based instead of cable-based. Even light bulbs are constantly being updated. Now you can install a light that has a speaker in it and control it with your phone. Be careful not to overinvest in a lot of electronics parts or rapidly changing technology, or you will end up with obsolete products no one wants.

Also, be wary of making custom products without first collecting a deposit. Otherwise, the customer might change his or her mind, and you will have sunk all this money into a product that no one else wants.

You can typically find someone who is still willing to purchase your outdated, obsolete inventory, but it's going to be at a deeply discounted price. You may even have to sell it at a loss.

MYTH #3: SHAREHOLDERS CAN ALWAYS PULL MONEY OUT OF THE BUSINESS WHEN NEEDED

Technically, if your business makes a profit, shareholders *should* be able to take a distribution of the earnings. However, if that profit is all tied up in your receivables, there won't be any money for shareholders to actually take their dividends.

Alternatively, if your business isn't making a profit, then any money pulled out is an *advance* on earnings, not a distribution of earnings. These advances are considered assets, but if the shareholders can't repay these advances, they're not truly assets.

Continually pulling money out of your business to finance your lifestyle even when the business isn't making a profit is a bad habit to develop. If your business isn't generating enough profit to support your lifestyle, you need to make some lifestyle changes until your business's profit increases.

MYTH #4: INVENTORY AND RECEIVABLES ARE AS GOOD AS CASH IN THE BANK

As already discussed, inventory can lose value, and accounts receivable may not be collectable. As such, they are not as good as cash in the bank.

Plus, cash is immediately liquid. If you want to invest in

$20,000 of new equipment and you have $20,000 in the bank, you simply go out and buy the equipment you want. If you instead have $20,000 sitting in inventory and accounts receivable, you have to first sell off inventory or collect on accounts receivable before you can purchase the new equipment. By the time you liquidate those assets, maybe you can't get the original deal of $20,000 for the equipment and now have to pay $25,000.

For your assets to be as useful as cash in the bank, they have to hold their value and be quickly liquidated. If you follow the tips I suggest in this chapter, you should be able to liquidate inventory and receivables quickly, making them almost as good as cash in the bank.

BEST PRACTICES: HOW TO KEEP ACCOUNTS RECEIVABLE UP TO DATE

THINK ABOUT HOW YOU SELL YOUR SERVICES

When you can, collect money at the time of the customer order. If you wait sixty days to bill customers and then give them ninety days to pay, that's five months before you get paid. Such a delay will create significant hiccups in your cash flow, and you will have to pay for all the expenses of the sale before receiving any of the income. To help your customers be comfortable with the idea of paying a deposit or the full amount up front, offer them a money-back guarantee.

Instead of getting the money all up front, you can also spread the payments out, either in a subscription service or in an installment payment plan. Offer customers the option of enrolling in autopay, and keep a customer credit card on file as a failsafe backup so that if you don't get paid by x date—say, within fifteen days of invoicing—you can go ahead and charge their card proactively. These strategies will help limit the risk of holding on to receivables that aren't getting paid.

As the business owner, you want to retain as much control over how and when you get paid as you can. If you leave it up to the customer to pay after the fact, you lose control. So either get at least some portion of the money up front or spread out the payments for a steady cash flow, and always keep a form of payment from the customer on file as a backup.

SET UP A STRICT PROCESS FOR PAYMENT

When it comes to getting payment, you want to get the clock rolling as soon as possible. Define payment terms at the time the customer places the order, and get invoices out quickly, within twenty-four hours of the sale.

Start following up with the customer even before the payment is late. If you give customers fifteen days to pay after invoicing, then on day fourteen, you should send a reminder. Don't just invoice and wait for customers to pay you. I used to do that for a lot of my clients, but I found out that almost 95% of the time, a follow-up phone call about the status of the payment was required to actually get paid.

If the bill isn't paid on day fifteen, call again on day sixteen. Follow up again on day twenty-one and day twenty-six and on and on until you're paid. If the customer makes a promise to pay, get them to commit to a specific date and then follow up on that date. You have to show the same follow-through that you would if you were trying to create a sale, because the payment is where you realize the value of the sale. If you don't collect the money, it wasn't really a sale.

Work with your customers if they're struggling to pay. Oftentimes, customers get overwhelmed because they can't pay the whole invoice right now. If you help them manage their cash flow by offering a payment plan, it will benefit your cash flow too, so help and be helped. Let's say they owe you $5,000 and can't afford to pay it all at once. You could offer them an interest-free plan where you charge their card $1,000 a week for the next five weeks. These payments are much more manageable, and many customers will agree to such a payment plan, especially if you don't charge them interest. If you get them to agree to such a plan, set it up with automatic card charges, so they can't miss payments.

Sometimes, though, you will need to cut off certain customers. If they're not paying you, they're not a customer. If you've tried to work with them but they won't or can't follow through on payment terms, then they're not a good customer for you. You can't keep extending them more credit and providing them with more products and services for no payment. You need to move on and find a new sale.

HAVE FIRM POLICIES FOR TRACKING CUSTOMER ORDERS

Sometimes the issue preventing you from collecting on receivables is not lack of customer payment but an issue with fulfillment of the order. To prevent such hang-ups, develop a policy for following up on the completion of customer orders, including tracking procurement of materials.

Say you own a lighting distribution company, and a customer ordered a special fixture from you that you don't normally stock. You order the fixture from your vendor, and you invoice your customer, with payment due upon receipt of the product.

Maybe it turns out that this item is back-ordered, and three weeks go by without shipment—that's three weeks without payment. Instead of waiting for the customer to eventually call and inquire about the status of their order, you should provide status updates along the way and periodically pull reports that will help you identify any issues. This way, you can discover the back-order early on and proactively solve the problem. For example, perhaps you can offer an alternative item that you have in stock. This will help you get payment faster and will also create an indelible impression with the customer.

Planning ahead and tracking orders will help you stop small bumps in the road from becoming major issues.

BEST PRACTICES: HOW TO EFFECTIVELY TRACK AND MANAGE INVENTORY

HAVE A SYSTEM IN PLACE TO TRACK INVENTORY

The first step to managing your inventory is having a system that tracks your inventory. Keep track of all product orders, and track all product sales in your point-of-sale system. Combined, these numbers will tell you what you should have in your inventory at any given time. I also recommend using a scanning system, where you scan every single item that physically enters or leaves inventory. This way, you're not just tracking ordered and sold products but also the products that have actually been received from suppliers and the products that have actually been pulled from storage to go to a customer.

BE ORGANIZED

You absolutely must keep your inventory organized. Your storage areas should be clean and well labeled so that you know what you have and how much you have. Keep a list of where each item is stored so you don't waste valuable time searching for a specific item. You should also try to keep different units of a single item in one place as much as possible. If you have some units of item A in bin 4, some in the back warehouse on shelf F, some in the showroom, and a whole package of them sitting in the corner unpacked, you're going to have a much harder time keeping track of the total amount than if you had all of them in one place.

LIMIT VARIETY AND QUANTITY OF ITEMS

Less is more when it comes to inventory. Recently, I've noticed even my grocery store adopting a leaner model for inventory. Before, cookies and crackers used to take up one side of an entire aisle. Now they take up only half of one side of an aisle, as the store is stocking fewer varieties and less of each type of variety.

You want to keep tight, lean inventory controls. Start by stocking a limited number of product types. When you have fewer SKUs, it is easier to store and track inventory. If you have hundreds of different SKUs, your salespeople could get confused about similar products. For example, if you have four different LED light bulbs, your salespeople could easily mix them up.

Then only stock the quantities that are needed in the next ninety days. There is so much helpful software out there now to tell you how many units of a product you're selling, and you can use this information to order accurate numbers of inventory. Plus, with the advances in technology, distribution, and shipping, you can often get products for customers quickly if you need more, so there's no need to be stocking more than what you can sell in the immediate future. If you work with inventory that may become out of date quickly, such as computer equipment and other rapidly changing technology, keep only enough on hand to immediately fulfill orders.

For special-order items, you don't need to keep stock on hand at all. Simply have the items delivered directly to the customer. There might be a delay of a couple of days to account for shipping, but this way, you won't be stuck with rarely ordered products gathering dust in storage.

In an ideal situation, if you work out preferential terms with your suppliers so that you don't have to pay until ninety days after the invoice date, you will get your inventory, sell it, and then use that money to pay for the inventory. This way, you don't need to front any large expenses yourself.

Shoot for working on a minimum inventory level with products that can move quickly. Focus on stocking your top sellers. Inventory is an investment and isn't immediately convertible to cash, so be smart about what you stock.

DO CYCLE COUNTS

Periodically, you want to physically count your inventory to make sure the actual numbers match up with the projected numbers. If you ordered ten items and sold six, you want to make sure you really do have four items sitting in inventory.

Full-scale inventory counts are often inaccurate, though. Trying to count everything at once is overwhelming, and you're basically guaranteed to make mistakes, as there's only so much counting a person can do in a day! Counting can get boring fast and isn't very much fun, so employees can easily lose their focus and may end up rushing to try to finish.

Instead of a yearly full-scale inventory count, do periodic cycle counts throughout the year, where you count just a certain subset of inventory. Maybe you count items 1–10 this week, items 11–19 next week, and items 20–29 the following week. Another benefit of cycle counting over full-scale inventories is you can focus on your most critical inventory items—your top sellers and your most expensive items. You still want to periodically count everything, but you can count the critical items more often.

Whenever you do inventory, the person doing the actual counting should *not* know how much of the item there should be. If you're expecting to get a certain number, you are more likely to get that number. You will get more accurate counts if you go into them blind, with no expected number already in your mind.

KEEP INVENTORY MOVING

You want to make sure your inventory is constantly moving. Monitor your sales data so that you can adjust accordingly. Maybe you used to sell two hundred of a certain product every month, but now you're selling only one hundred. You need to adjust your inventory numbers in response.

Keep an eye on high-dollar items in particular. You can afford to make more mistakes with low-cost products than high-cost ones. If you accidentally order one hundred units of a $1 product that you don't need, that's only $100. If you order one hundred unneeded units of a $100 product, though, that's $10,000.

The quicker you can turn your inventory, the better, but

sometimes you might have a surplus. Maybe you sold a hundred light bulbs last week, so you bought a hundred for this week, too, but then sold only twenty. That's not the end of the world, but you don't want to hold on to that inventory for a long time either. If you have inventory that's been sitting for more than ninety days, create sales programs and offer discounts to keep the inventory moving.

A lot of entrepreneurs get it stuck in their heads that they should get x dollars for something, and they won't accept anything less. For instance, I had a client who bought a commercial building in 2005 and was dead set on getting $30 a square foot as the lease rate. He didn't lease it right away, and then the market turned. The building was in an area that was hard hit by the recession. Different businesses approached him to lease the space for far less than he wanted—around $7 to $10 a square foot—and he refused. He ended up with just one tenant in a small portion of the building paying the $30 a square foot he wanted.

I kept telling him, "Lease the space for less. Just do a shorter-term lease, and at least you'll have some money coming in. Something is better than nothing." He refused. It was $30 a square foot or nothing for him. He *finally* leased it in 2017, but for more than ten years, he held that building basically empty. In that time, he didn't have a dime of profit coming in, as the little income he was receiving from the lone tenant went entirely to the taxes and maintenance of the building. When you do the math, had he leased it for $7 a square foot, he would have doubled his money over the ten years.

Sometimes you might have to accept less for something than you want. Be open and flexible. Maybe you can't get $10 for this product today but can get $8. That might cut your profit margin down to $2 a unit versus $4, but if you move that inventory out, you can replace it with some other product that your customers are more interested in having. You will make less of a margin per product, but you'll make more money overall in the long term. If you want to get rid of slow-moving inventory, try to do it in bulk. This way, you can save money on shipping costs and labor and hopefully make up for the narrowed profit margin.

The most important thing is to maintain traction and keep rolling forward. If you let inventory sit too long, you may be forced to sell below cost, and then you're making no margin.

ACQUISITION OF ASSETS AND DEPRECIATION

Nearly every noncash asset—whether it's a piece of equipment, a building, or even goodwill—has a certain life span and depreciates over time as you use it.

DEPRECIATION AND TAXES

When you're acquiring assets, you have to keep in mind how that asset will be depreciated for both tax purposes and financial reporting purposes, as the two might be very different.

For tax purposes, the IRS has a variety of regulations you must follow regarding how different items can be amortized and depreciated—for example, the IRS specifies certain depreciation rates and useful life spans for different types of assets. These guidelines will limit how much of an asset you can expense in a year. For financial reporting purposes, though, you can choose to use different time lines and list expenses differently.

For example, let's say you spend $100,000 to furnish your office. For tax purposes, you can expense all of that in a single year to save on taxes. However, those furnishings will still be an asset for seven years. To reflect that, for book purposes, use straight-line depreciation on the asset's value on the balance sheet over seven years. So each year, the asset value will go down by $14,286. That amount goes on your P&L as an expense. Doing this will make your books look better and make your business look more consistently profitable. If you don't do this, you will show very low profit the year you purchase the furnishings and then higher profit for every year after, which is not an accurate reflection of your business's true annual profit.

You should treat intangible assets in a similar way. If you acquire a new franchise, you might have to pay a $250,000 franchise fee up front. That fee is considered goodwill for tax purposes, so you are required to amortize it over fifteen years. For financial statement purposes, though, you will amortize the fee over the term of the franchise. If it's a five-year agreement, you will amortize it over five years. If it's a twenty-five-year agreement, you will amortize it over twenty-five years.

I personally find the goodwill-amortization rule ridiculous. Let's take a five-year $250,000 franchise fee as an example. You're not allowed to expense more than one-fifteenth of it each year, so you can deduct only $16,667 each year. In reality, though, and for book purposes, the true expense is $50,000. So not only do your books look worse, showing lower profit, but you also end up with a greater taxable profit and thus have to pay more in tax. Because of this, when you purchase an asset, especially an intangible one, you must plan ahead and have an adequate reserve on hand to cover any tax liabilities associated with the acquisition.

REPAIR OR REPLACE?

In today's day and age, it may cost the same (or more) to fix something than to replace it. As such, part of your asset-acquisition strategy must include guidelines on whether to repair or replace an item.

For example, at eeCPA, if a computer can't be fixed in one repair session, we buy a new one instead. After analyzing the cost of our internal downtime and the cost of having a professional IT person come out to do the repair, we've found that if the repair takes more than one service call, buying a new computer will save us money over trying to get the old one working again.

Make sure that you're spending money in a way that will produce a return for you—sometimes that means maintaining equipment, and sometimes it means investing in new equipment.

KEY TIPS

- **Remember that your assets only have value if you can convert them to cash.** Sometimes you won't be able to sell certain inventory or won't be able to collect on certain receivables. In that case, you can't count on these assets to produce cash flow.
- **Start following up on receivables immediately, and offer payment plans when needed.** Receivables should not go unpaid for more than ninety days. Work with your customers. If you make it easier for them to pay you by offering payment plans and autopay options, the sooner you will get your money.
- **Keep inventory moving.** The longer your inventory sits, the greater the chance of it becoming out of date.

Keep a high turnover rate to ensure all your inventory on hand has true value. Sometimes you will need to be flexible and offer items at a discount just to get them sold.

CHAPTER 9

CUTTING YOUR LOSSES

HOW MUCH DO YOU OWE?

The next part of the balance sheet is current and long-term liabilities—or everything you owe and haven't paid for yet. Your liabilities include a multitude of various debts that are often overlooked or misunderstood.

Here's an example of what the liabilities portion of your balance sheet might look like:

Excerpt Service Liabilities

	12/31/17	12/31/16	Change
Current Liabilities			
Accounts Payable	294,096	-	294,096
Total Accounts Payable	294,096	-	294,096
American Express Gold 2	-	255	(255)
Chase Ink Card 2	744	15,164	(14,420)
Total Credit Cards	744	15,419	(14,675)
Arizona Department of Revenue Payable	750		750
Payroll Liabilities	13,531	901	12,630
Wells Fargo Line of Credit	125,000		125,000
Current Portion of Long-Term Debt	11,254		11,254
Total Other Current Liabilities	150,535	901	149,634
Total Current Liabilities	**445,375**	**16,320**	**429,054**
Long-Term Liabilities			
Tenant Security Deposit	11,625		11,625
US Bank Loan: Audi	54,220		54,220
Less Current Portion of Long-Term Debt	*(11,254)*		*(11,254)*
Total Long-Term Liabilities	**54,590**	-	**54,590**
Total Liabilities	**499,965**	**16,320**	**483,645**

LIABILITIES

CURRENT LIABILITIES

Current liabilities are liabilities that are due within a year. They include accounts payable, credit card debt, payroll liabilities, taxes, incurred expenses that haven't been paid yet, lines of credit, and loans.

- **Accounts payable**—Your accounts payable is all the money you owe to your vendors. Often, you will get materials from suppliers and won't have to pay for up to ninety days. For the duration of that time, the amount you owe to your vendors sits on your balance sheet as a liability.
- **Credit cards**—Until you pay off the balance on your credit cards, it is a current liability. If you use a credit card to pay your vendors, you no longer owe your vendors, but you still owe that money to the credit card company.
- **Payroll liabilities**—There are a lot of laws and rules around taking money out of an employee's pay. Your payroll liabilities include everything from taxes to garnishment of wages for child support to 401(k) contributions. Basically, any money that is taken out of an employee's paycheck and is supposed to go somewhere else is a liability until you actually put the money where it is supposed to go.
- **Taxes**—All the taxes you owe that you haven't paid yet are also liabilities. The most important taxes to focus on are your income taxes, your property taxes (which are usually fairly substantial for businesses), and your sales tax. For your tax liabilities, you need to know not only how much you owe but also *when* you owe it. A lot of taxes accrue over time and must be paid in one large lump sum, so it is especially important to keep track of these liabilities.

- **Incurred but unpaid expenses**—Any expenses you've incurred that haven't been paid are liabilities. So perhaps you hire a subcontractor and they complete the work but haven't invoiced you yet. Or perhaps for tax purposes you expensed a bunch of employee bonuses before the year's end before actually paying for them. Because those expenses—the contracted work or bonuses—still need to be paid, they're liabilities.
- **Lines of credit**—When you take an advance from a line of credit, you have to repay that, so it's a liability. A lot of companies keep track of only the interest they owe on a line of credit, as that's all they have to pay in the short term. However, if you're not paying down the principal of your line of credit frequently, the bank will eventually term out the loan, and you will have to start making monthly principal and interest payments instead of just interest payments. So it is important for you to keep track of the full liability of the line of credit, not just the interest.
- **Loans**—All the payments you owe within the next year for loans, such as vehicle or equipment loans, are current liabilities.

LONG-TERM LIABILITIES

Long-term liabilities are liabilities that are not due within the next year. The most common long-term liabilities are long-term loans. The amount of the loan due within the next year is a current liability, while the remaining portion of the loan is a long-term liability. The interest on the debt is typically classified as an operating expense.

So to use the example from the liabilities excerpt at the start of the chapter, say you have an Audi car loan of $54,220. That amount is listed as a long-term liability ("US Bank Loan—Audi"). Then, underneath that line on the balance sheet, you list the current liability of the loan, or the amount you are going to pay on the loan in the coming year ("Less Current Portion of Long-Term Debt"), which is $12,000. That leaves a total of $42,220 in the long-term liabilities. The $12,000 current liability is also listed in the current liabilities section, as "Current Portion of Long-Term Debt."

Current Portion of LT Debt

	12/31/17	12/31/16	Change
Other Current Liabilities			
Arizona Department of Revenue Payable	750		750
Payroll Liabilities	13,531	901	12,630
Wells Fargo Line of Credit	125,000		125,000
Current Portion of Long-Term Debt	11,254		11,254
Total Other Current Liabilities	150,535	901	149,634
Long-Term Liabilities			
Tenant Security Deposit	11,625		11,625
US Bank Loan: Audi	54,220		54,220
Less Current Portion of Long-Term Debt	(11,254)		(11,254)
Total Long-Term Liabilities	54,590	-	54,590

Listing the loan in this way accurately shows both the current and the long-term liabilities associated with the loan.

COMMON MISCONCEPTIONS ABOUT LIABILITIES
MYTH #1: CUSTOMER DEPOSITS ARE INCOME

A lot of people record customer deposits as income, but if you haven't done the work yet—if you haven't incurred and paid for the corresponding expenses—a customer deposit is a liability, not income. You took money from the customer and have an obligation to fulfill the sale—that is, you still owe the customer something that you haven't delivered. Once you complete the work, then you can record that deposit as income.

Recording customer deposits as income can result in overstated profit, because none of the expenses have been recognized yet, and that means more taxes for you. One of my clients, an interior designer, got $750,000 of customer deposits in December 2017 for upcoming work in 2018. In total, she will incur expenses of around $600,000 in 2018 related to those deposits. In 2017, though, she originally recorded the $750,000 as income, making it seem as if she'd made $750,000 in profit, when in reality her profit is going to end up being $150,000. We reclassified those deposits for her and saved her from paying taxes on profit she didn't really make.

Treating customer deposits as income instead of liabilities can result not only in overpaying taxes but also in accumulating unmanageable amounts of debt. If you misuse customer deposits as income, you could find yourself inadvertently involved in a pyramid scheme, such as the Bernie Madoff scandal.

Back in 2008, Scott Coles of Mortgages Limited found himself in just such a scandal in Phoenix. He collected investments from people, with a promise to pay 10% interest, and then he invested the money in various prominent and high-end real estate development projects (for example, skyscraper office buildings and the like) in Tempe and Phoenix. He paid out the interest he'd promised investors, no problem.

Then the real estate market turned. Suddenly, he found himself strapped for cash. So he began misappropriating customer deposits, using them to fuel previous jobs. Let's say he took a deposit from Suzy that was supposed to be for a project in Tempe. Well, work hadn't started yet on the Tempe project, and meanwhile he was running short on money for a Phoenix project, so he would take Suzy's deposit and use it for the Phoenix job.

You should use a customer's deposit only for their particular project, not for any other purpose. Sometimes you might be able to get away with using a customer deposit for a different, currently cash-strapped project, but what happens if there's a downturn or something that prevents you from completing your projects? Using real estate as an example, maybe a property doesn't sell for what you expect, or maybe your contractor walks off the job. Now you don't have the money to fulfill your customer's project, and you can't refund them their deposit either, as you've already spent it.

This is what happened to Scott Coles with the real estate recession. All of a sudden, there was no more demand for this kind of real estate, and there was no way he was going to be able to lease the spaces. He didn't have enough funds lined up, so the projects failed and stopped midstream.

He was deep underwater, with no way to pay back the money he owed to his investors. Soon, he couldn't even make the interest payments anymore, and the whole mess was uncovered. Some people had invested a significant portion of their holdings with him—in some cases, their entire life savings. For the first few years, they were very pleased about getting their 10% returns because at the time the interest rate was only 1%–2% if you left your money in the bank. But then they lost everything. Coles ended up committing suicide because he couldn't face all his investors.

You must be careful with how you treat customer deposits, or you can soon be out of business or in a really bad position with your customers. If you start using one customer's deposit for a different customer's job, you have to save up money to repay the deposit if needed for any reason. You're like a trustee when you accept a deposit from a customer. The money is given to you in trust as a deposit for a project, and segregating those funds is critical.

MYTH #2: EQUIPMENT LEASES ARE AS GOOD AS TRADITIONAL BANK LOANS

In the healthcare profession and construction especially, you need to invest quite a bit in equipment, and many people choose to lease the equipment (with the option to purchase it at the end of the term) to spread the cost out over time. In many cases, it would make more sense financially for them to take out a loan to purchase the equipment than to lease it, but often they go with the lease because they don't want to deal with the loan process and think the two liabilities are the same.

Leasing can be much more expensive, though, because the imputed lease rate is much higher than the interest rate on a traditional loan—it is often 20%-30% of the total cost of the equipment. For example, say you lease a $200,000 piece of equipment over seven years with a 20% imputed lease rate. That means you're going to pay an extra $173,000 total over the term (for a total of $373,000) versus if you got a 7% loan, you would pay only $53,500 in interest, for a total of $253,500.

The differential there is $119,500 over a seven-year term—an extra $17,000 a year or more than $1,400 extra each month. Even if the process of taking out the loan instead of leasing cost you $5,000 plus another $5,000 for your accountant's fees, you would recoup those costs in the first year and still save $110,000 just by going through the process of a traditional bank loan versus an equipment lease loan.

When you take on a liability, such as an equipment lease or a traditional bank loan, you need to look at the full long-term liability you're signing up for, as it might be costing you more money than you realize. Making smart decisions about how you take on debt can reduce your overall liabilities.

PAYROLL LIABILITIES

Payroll liabilities are often the biggest liability you will face. Payroll liabilities are all the funds you collect out of your employees' paycheck for a multitude of different reasons and then must remit to the appropriate entity, whether it's the government, a health insurance company, or a 401(k) company. To add to the liability, you also have to match many of those funds. For example, you have to match Social Security and Medicare taxes dollar for dollar, and depending on your company's policy, you may have to match 401(k) contributions up to a certain amount.

Keeping careful track of these liabilities and making sure all these payments are actually made is critical because surprises in this area can cause serious problems for your employees. If an employee's check is garnished for child support, for example, and you don't get that money to the right place, you're going to be creating major problems for that employee and his child.

Not paying these liabilities on time can also cause a lot of problems for you as the employer. Failure to comply in this area is very serious to the government. For example, if you withhold funds for 401(k) contributions and then don't get that money to the 401(k) investment company within seven days, per the Department of Labor, you will be subject to penalties that can be very steep, up to $1,500 per day for noncompliance.

In fact, even if you have an LLC, file for bankruptcy, and close the business down, if you withheld funds from an employee's paycheck and didn't turn that money over to the government, you will be assessed a trust fund penalty, which is about 50% of the money that was withheld and not turned over. This penalty will be attached to your personal income tax record as the business owner, and it won't go away.

The government will make sure you pay these liabilities eventually and will charge hefty fines in the process, so stay on top of these liabilities to avoid additional penalties.

TAX LIABILITIES

You need to keep careful track of all your various tax liabilities because taxes tend to accrue over time to be paid once or twice a year in large lump sums. If you don't keep track, you might not have the money needed to pay the bill when it comes due, and then you'll be in hot water. You have to stay on top of all the different taxes and their unique payment schedules.

PAYROLL TAXES

Payroll taxes, depending on the amount, are usually due on a semiweekly basis, and you have to pay them within three days of the payroll date. If you process payroll on Friday, then the taxes are due Wednesday.

INCOME TAX

While you file income tax annually, you have to make quarterly estimated payments throughout the year. Estimated tax payments for C-corps are due in April, June, September, and December, and individual estimated taxes are due April, June, September, and January.

The penalty for not paying estimated taxes is essentially an interest charge—just 4% currently but subject to change as interest rates change. So in some cases, if you really need the funds and can make more money by using them now instead of paying your estimated taxes, choosing to not pay and take the penalty can be a smart business decision. In a way, it's like you're using the money as a preapproved loan. You definitely want to continue keeping track of how much you owe, including the added 4% penalty, though, as you will have to pay this money eventually. You have until your tax return is due, in March or April the following year, to pay the total tax amount plus penalty.

A rough estimate of your income tax liability is 40% of the profit from your P&L. This amount is a decent base reserve to have. The actual tax liability will of course vary depending on your particular income tax rate and any additional taxes that might apply. For example, Texas has a franchise tax that isn't based on income. I encourage my clients to keep this 40-percent-of-profit reserve in a money market account to help keep the reserve intact while also earning some interest.

While the penalty for not paying estimated taxes is a very reasonable 4%, if you're late paying the taxes and penalty in March or April, then the penalties become much more significant. If you file late, there is a 5% late fee each month you don't file (with a cap at 25% of your total due taxes), and for every month without payment, there is an additional 0.5% fee (again with a cap of 25%). These penalties can add up fairly quickly. If you don't file or pay your taxes for five months, you will end up paying 27.5% of your total taxes due as a penalty. The late-filing penalty is where you get hit especially hard, so even if you can't pay your taxes, you should still at least file, to avoid the 5%-per-month late-filing penalty assessment.

SALES TAX

Sales tax is typically due monthly, quarterly, or annually, depending on which state you're in and how much sales tax you're collecting. If you're collecting less than $1,000 of sales tax a year in any state, you're probably going to pay annually, unless you're selling alcohol, which the federal government regulates, in which case you have to submit reports every month, even if you collected only a dollar in sales tax.

If you collect sales tax in multiple states, you will have to keep track of and pay all the state tax bills separately. For a client of ours that sells wine nationwide, for example, we typically file twenty-nine different monthly sales tax reports because they sell wine in twenty-nine different states.

The sales tax rates can vary by state and even locality. Here in Scottsdale, the sales tax rate is 7.95%. If I go across the street to Phoenix, I'm going to pay 8.6%. So if I need to purchase a lot of supplies from Home Depot,

I'm better off going to the one in Scottsdale, because I'll save 0.65%.

PROPERTY TAX

Property taxes are typically due once or twice a year, with the due date varying depending on the state. For example, if you fail to pay property taxes in Arizona, you will be obligated to pay 16% interest on the late payments and could risk losing your property.

A lot of people here in Phoenix simply don't pay their property taxes. After a year or two of nonpayment, the county auctions off those debts. By selling the debt to the general public, they recoup a portion of that debt immediately instead of waiting and hoping to collect the full property tax owed. As the property owner who hasn't paid the taxes, you are still liable for the full amount, and if you don't pay the lien that has been sold to someone else, you can lose your whole property.

For example, maybe you have a $1 million commercial property, and the taxes are $20,000 a year. Each time you're late on a payment, you will be charged interest at the rate of 16% per annum, prorated monthly. Now let's say you don't pay the taxes for three years, and the county sells the debt to someone else. Now, if you don't pay back the person who bought the debt, the property will go into foreclosure, and you will lose ownership to the person who owns the tax lien. For $60,000 (three years' worth of property taxes), plus interest, you could lose your $1 million property.

Obviously, it is pretty important to pay these taxes, but they can creep up on you. For example, in Arizona, the first property tax bill you receive for the year comes in September, with the taxes paid in arrears. So you could be sitting in your building for months before having to make any property tax payments.

STAY ON TOP OF YOUR TAXES

Your taxes are your taxes, and they're not going to go away. If you don't have the requisite expertise yourself, hire someone to help you keep on top of all these different due dates and amounts and also to help you plan ahead so you have the cash available to pay the bills.

THE DANGER OF TOO MANY LIABILITIES—NO MORE LOANS

If you have too many liabilities, no one's going to want to lend you more money.

Let's say you have a $30,000 car loan with US Bank, an $800,000 building loan with Bank of America, and a $150,000 line of credit you've drawn on with Wells Fargo. Total, let's say the current liabilities portion of all this debt is $120,000. Then that's $10,000 a month your business has to come up with above and beyond the operating expenses, such as payroll, rent, raw materials, and all the other costs of doing business.

This situation is why people often think they're making a profit and then are confused about why they don't have any cash. If you excluded all your debt liabilities in this example, then yes, you might be making a profit, but once you factor in the current liabilities obligation, that cash is depleted.

So now you find yourself in need of cash, but no bank is going to give you a loan, because you already owe all this money to other people. All your assets already have debts and liens against them, so the bank will have no collateral to issue you a loan.

Be careful about taking on too many liabilities, as it can impact your future ability to obtain loans.

RATIO OF CURRENT ASSETS TO CURRENT LIABILITIES

For day-to-day operations, you will typically be most concerned with current assets and liabilities, as you need your current assets to outweigh your current liabilities in order to run a profit. Long-term assets and liabilities are also important to know, though, for making long-term strategic decisions.

Typically, you want current assets to exceed current liabilities, but during periods of change or growth, this can flip-flop. Sometimes you will deplete your current assets while also taking on a lot of current liabilities in order to invest in long-term assets. For example, at eeCPA, I'm moving and setting up a new office in addition to making significant marketing investments. I've used up most of my cash reserves as well as my line of credit so I could invest in these long-term assets.

As a result, I have fewer current assets and more current liabilities than normal. This kind of financial picture is OK for only short periods associated with growth or change of some kind. As soon as I'm done setting up the new office, my immediate goal will be to refinance my debt and replenish my current cash assets. In this way, I will get my balance sheet back to a healthier spot, with my current assets outweighing my current liabilities. Making these changes will help me to withstand future hits that may potentially come my way.

If you're making large long-term investments in your business, such as infrastructure, equipment, fixed assets, or even intellectual property, sometimes you have to take on current liabilities and use current assets to fund those investments, but you want to pay back your current liabilities and replenish your current assets as quickly as possible.

BEST PRACTICES: HOW TO TRACK AND MANAGE CURRENT LIABILITIES
ACCOUNTS PAYABLE

You absolutely must track your accounts payable. Think back to that horror story at the solar company where the bookkeeper wasn't putting the bills in the system, resulting in a huge amount of debt that completely took the business owner by surprise. To prevent such surprises, record invoices into the system daily or weekly.

You also can't rely on your vendors to properly invoice you and follow up regarding payment. Some vendors and consultants are notorious for sitting on invoices for months before finally sending them.

You don't necessarily need to be hounding your vendors to send you invoices, but you need to estimate and keep track of what those bills will be so that you're not stuck with a surprise payment in another two, three, or four months. Otherwise, you might forget that you owe $5,000 to a certain vendor and spend that money on a marketing campaign. Then, when the vendor finally sends the invoice, you have to try to scrounge $5,000 up out of nowhere.

CREDIT CARDS

A lot of people wait until they get their credit bill and then they look through the charges. Instead, you should link your credit card charges directly to your accounting system. Once the charges are in your accounting system, you can categorize them accordingly and keep a running balance of what you owe. This way, you will know exactly what to expect when you get the bill at the end of the month.

When you track the charges daily instead of monthly, you can also more quickly spot unusual spending, whether it's potential fraud, a product price increase you weren't notified of, an employee exceeding the allotted spending limits, or anything else.

You should pay off your credit cards in full each month, as the interest rates are hefty, often 20% or more. If you need to borrow money for an extended time, get a loan or a line of credit instead, where you will instead be paying closer to 6%–7% interest.

AUTO-RENEWALS

From streaming services to spas to even accounting firms like eeCPA, pay-by-the month subscription services are becoming popular. Lots of software especially is now billed by the month. You need to watch out for auto-renewals to ensure you're not paying for services you're not using anymore. Keep a list of what your subscriptions are and what they cost, and periodically review the list to find any services you might have forgotten to cancel.

Even contracts might have auto-renewal provisions. You should know when automatic contract renewals are coming up so that you can renegotiate price or terms as appropriate. If you're not tracking the auto-renewal date, you could be stuck under contract to pay a certain amount over a period, and that's a huge liability.

For example, I was recently surprised by a new insurance bill. Most commercial insurance is tied to your sales or payroll, and if you're in growth mode, both your sales and payroll will be increasing year over year. Then, all of a sudden, as happened to me, you're whacked with an insurance bill double the normal amount.

Keep track of any expected price increases in your various subscription-based payments, so that you can adjust your budget accordingly, and monitor all auto-renewals. If you want to rebid or potentially find a different company for a certain service or product, set an alert sixty days in advance of the renewal date. You often need these services to remain in business, so you want to be sure to give yourself enough time to negotiate for better terms or get set up at a new company.

VENDOR TERMS

Obviously, you want to work out the best terms you can with your vendors. My personal philosophy is to pay everything as quickly as I can, because I don't like to carry large amounts of debt. Sometimes, though, there will be times when you simply don't have the cash flow to pay your debts right away. For these times, having good terms with your vendors will help you stretch your money without having to get a bank loan or use a credit card to finance your business.

If you need help with cash flow, try to establish terms where you get sixty to ninety days to pay after invoicing. If you previously had to pay a vendor within ten days but are able to extend that to sixty days, you've just bought yourself free financing for those fifty days. Especially when you're purchasing products for resale, this longer payment time line can make a huge difference. If your customers typically pay you within thirty days, then with sixty-day payment terms, you can wait until you collect from your customers before you pay your vendors.

Alternatively, you can choose to pay vendors or subcontractors quickly in return for service benefits. People like getting paid quickly, so they will often give priority to those clients who pay the fastest.

Once you establish terms, stay true to them. Your vendors may be willing to extend terms even further to help you out in a tough time, but if you can't keep to the established contract, they're not going to give you the best pricing. The best pricing is for the customers who are reliable and pay on time.

UTILITIES

Unlike many other current liabilities, utilities usually can't be negotiated. As a result, you have to be careful with these bills, especially when dealing with seasonal utility spikes. Here in Arizona, summer utility costs are three to four times higher than in the winter because of the AC required, and in areas with harsh winters, winter utility costs will skyrocket due to the heat needed.

If you can't pay your utilities, your services will get cut off, and then your business won't be able to function. So plan ahead for utility spikes.

RESERVES

Keep a base minimum of cash in your account to cover any contingencies, such as forgotten expenses or unexpected emergency spending. A solid baseline, as detailed in chapter 7, is one month of payroll for service companies or one month of payroll plus one month of average purchases for retail companies.

You also always want to have a line of credit available to you for emergencies. If you max out your line of credit, talk to the bank about terming that line of credit out (essentially converting it to a loan) so you can then open a new line of credit for emergencies. (This is what I plan to do because I had to max out my line of credit to cover moving expenses.) It is always best to start talking to your bank sooner rather than later. You want to set up adequate cash and line of credit reserves before you get into a position where you have no cash at all.

KEY TIPS

- **Have a reliable system of tracking liabilities.** If you have $100,000 in cash and $120,000 in unpaid bills, you're in debt. If you're not properly tracking your liabilities, you may spend money you think you have but really don't, like Robert, the CEO of the solar company who wound up with $250,000 of unexpected debt he had no way of paying.

- **Enter bills into your system immediately.** Even if you plan on paying a bill later, enter it into your system as soon as you get it. Bills need to be entered daily or weekly so that you have an accurate financial picture of your business.

CHAPTER 10

BUILDING EQUITY

WHAT IS YOUR EQUITY?

The last part of the balance sheet is equity. Here's an excerpt of what that portion of the balance sheet might look like for a service company:

Excerpt Service Equity

	12/31/17	12/31/16	Change
Equity			
Capital Stock	1,000	1,000	-
Retained Earnings	272,337	449,027	(176,690)
Shareholder Distributions	-	(166,850)	166,850
Taxes	-	(1,700)	1,700
Total Shareholder Distributions	-	(168,550)	168,550
Net Income	163,759	(8,141)	171,900
Total Equity	**437,096**	**273,337**	**163,759**

BUILDING EQUITY · 231

TO PARTNER OR NOT TO PARTNER—THE IMPORTANCE OF EQUITY

Before getting into business with anyone—whether it's a partnership, LLC, S corp, or C corp—you want to start with a clear understanding of what each person is bringing in, what they're expecting to get out, and how the business partnership is going to work from a financial perspective.

One day, my long-term client Tina came in with her best friend, Cassandra, for a consultation about a partnership. Cassandra owned a combination café–gift shop in a public park in Alaska and also was responsible for providing a person to collect the entrance fee at the gate to the park. After the one-year contract with the park was up, Cassandra wanted to bring in Tina, who was currently an employee at the gift shop, as a partner, and then the two of them would relocate to Minnesota and open up a shop following the same model in a park there.

When Tina and Cassandra first came into my office, they thought they were totally on the same page and would make excellent partners. Then we sat down and had a discussion about the equity they each would be contributing. Tina had contributed quite a bit of shelving, furnishings to decorate the shop, and a lot of the shop's inventory. She managed the day-to-day needs of the shop, from arranging the cooking of the food to the ordering of supplies. Meanwhile, Cassandra had made a huge investment in the enterprise as well in refrigeration equipment and additional shelving units.

These items would be their equity in the new business, so we needed to determine the fair market value of these things. We also needed to figure out how to equalize their contributions, as they wanted to be fifty-fifty partners. Rarely does any partnership start with an equal fifty-fifty contribution of equity unless you're dealing only with cash investments. With basically any startup, even if you don't have furnishings or physical items to consider, like Tina and Cassandra, you still have to consider sweat equity—the differences in the work each person will be contributing to the business.

Because Tina and Cassandra wanted to share profits fifty-fifty, we had to figure out a way to first repay whichever of them was making the larger initial equity investment. As we began tallying up their contributions, the disagreements began. Cassandra insisted her furnishings were newer and cost more, while Tina argued that her furnishings weren't "old" but antiques and thus had a higher value than Cassandra's furnishings.

As we discussed everything that needed to happen to launch this new business, I could see Cassandra's face and body language shift. She was clearly changing her mind about the whole partnership. She didn't feel as if Tina's contributions were enough to justify fifty-fifty profit sharing, even though she had fully agreed prior to the meeting that the partnership should be fifty-fifty. Tina also seemed more unsure about the partnership.

After the consultation, Tina and Cassandra decided not to move forward with the partnership, which I think was the best decision, especially for the sake of their friendship. The consultation cost them around $250 but saved them thousands of dollars in a failed partnership. If you don't have a clear understanding of how a business arrangement is going to work, not starting the business is the best thing in the long run. Having clear expectations and an understanding of who's going to handle what and assigning set values to each person's contribution is really important for sustainability of a business.

EQUITY

Equity is long-term invested funds in the business, plus any current/operating profits from the business, less any distributions or dividends that have been paid out to the members or shareholders in the enterprise. Unlike loans, equity investments are not required to be repaid over any certain amount of time, though some shareholders may receive a preferred return on their investment.

So on your balance sheet, you will have four main categories that increase the equity amount:

- capital investments from nonlending institutions (typically the money you invested to get the business started)
- retained earnings of the business
- money invested by members/shareholders (through the purchase of stock or, in the case of an LLC, units)
- net income (the year's profit)

And you will have one main category that reduces your equity:

- shareholder distributions or dividends paid out

The resulting net equity is what your net investment in the business is at any point in time. This net equity is also equivalent to your total assets minus your total liabilities.

Having positive equity is like having a rainy day fund or a crisis fund. It will allow you to withstand fluctuations in the economy and to take advantage of potential growth opportunities.

COMMON MISCONCEPTIONS ABOUT EQUITY
MYTH #1: WHO CARES? IT'S MY MONEY; I CAN TAKE IT OUT

Yes, you *can* take money out of your business, but you might not *want* to for several different reasons. Typically, you should only be distributing a percentage of the current earnings and reinvesting the remainder of the earnings in the business activities, or if the business isn't making a profit, you shouldn't be distributing earnings at all.

Negative Equity

The most important reason you might not want to take money out is that it could create negative equity for your business.

You want to have positive equity. If you have negative equity, it usually means either your business isn't profitable or the shareholders/members are withdrawing more than the current earnings of the business, which is a bad practice to get into.

If you want to sell your business, you definitely don't want to put it into a negative equity position, as it will make your business look unprofitable. When you're selling your business, it's just like going on a first date—you want to make the best first impression you can. Just as you'd get dressed up for a date, you want to dress up your business so it looks like a valuable investment. Positive equity is part of that.

It's the same if you want to get outside financing. You want your business to look its best. If you have negative equity in the business, it means your liabilities exceed your assets, and that will make lenders and investors wary.

Tax Consequences

Taking money out of your business could also trigger unexpected tax consequences for you.

Let's say you have an S corporation and this year you didn't make any profit. However, you got a new loan to provide working capital for the business, so you have cash in the bank. Normally, when you take a distribution of retained earnings from an S corporation, there is no tax effect. However, if you take out money in this situation, it is not considered a distribution of earnings, as the business did not have any earnings to distribute this year. Rather, you are redeeming your equity in the business. So the government sees that withdrawal as a sale of equity, which is subject to the capital gains tax. If you are in a low enough tax bracket that you don't have to pay capital gains tax, this won't matter, but most likely, you will be triggering a 15%–20% tax you otherwise wouldn't have to pay.

You must keep careful track of your equity on your balance sheet so that you don't accidentally overdraw and make a sale of equity when you just wanted a distribution of earnings, as this mistake can result in extra taxes.

If your business doesn't have earnings to distribute but you need to take money from the business, the best strategy is to classify the withdrawal as a shareholder loan. Then, in the future, when the business does make a profit, you can take out earnings and repay the loan. Taking out shareholder loans can be a slippery slope, though, so use this strategy sparingly.

Mixing of Personal and Business Expenses

A lot of business owners are bad about comingling business and personal expenses. This habit seems especially prevalent for those with businesses structured as flow-through entities, such as LLCs and S corporations. With flow-through entities, the business's income is passed through to the business owner and treated as their personal income. As a result, these business owners think, *My business's money is my money*, and then they use business funds as their personal bank account and charge personal items to the company credit card.

Obviously, you should never do this, because personal expenses—your home utility bills, your hair appointments, your personal massages, your babysitters, your pet food, and so on—are not business expenses.

When it comes to tax time, the easiest way to prevent these personal expenses from becoming an issue is to categorize them as distributions from the company. Making this classification is often necessary but also reduces your equity. It is important to keep business and personal separate to prevent this situation. Your business's money is your business's money, not your money.

MYTH #2: EQUITY IS SPLIT EQUALLY BETWEEN FIFTY-FIFTY PARTNERS

Many people believe that if partners in a business are splitting profits fifty-fifty, then the equity is also split equally between them, but this is rarely the case, especially in the case of partnerships with one money partner and one sweat partner. (Note that we're not talking about the entity structure of partnership but about any business partnership, be it an S corporation, LLC, or whatever.) You might split profits fifty-fifty, but the equity belongs to whoever contributed it.

With a money-and-sweat partnership, which is especially common in real estate development deals, one person is a silent partner who just contributes money and does no work. Meanwhile, the other person contributes no money or a much smaller amount of money, but this partner's feet are on the ground—he or she is choosing deals, negotiating, and putting in the sweat.

Business partnerships are a lot like marriages, and just like marriages, one of the biggest conflicts is money. I can't tell you how many business partners have come through my door fighting like a husband and wife over money.

Often, sweat partners feel as if they have earned more equity in the business because they're the ones doing all the work, but they forget that the business couldn't exist without the funding from their money partners. Meanwhile, money partners are acutely aware of how much money they've sunk into the business and think they have clearly invested more than their sweat partners. They may undervalue the amount of work the sweat partners are putting in.

There are often large discrepancies in both the perceived and real value each person in the relationship is bringing to the table, especially when trying to compare unlike things, such as money and sweat. To prevent damage to your business and your relationship with your partner, you need to clearly define the terms of your partnership from the onset, with an operating agreement.

BEST PRACTICES: HOW TO CREATE AN OPERATING AGREEMENT

You should absolutely invest in an operating agreement or at least a statement to lay out the framework for your partnership. A lot of people don't spend enough time on the operating agreement or go to an attorney who just follows a template, but it's worth it to spend a bit more time on this document. At the end of the day, when it comes time to sell or dissolve the business, you're going to split it out based on how the equity shares are defined in the operating agreement, so you don't want to cut corners here.

In your operating agreement, you should outline the following:

- Contributions
    - What is each member contributing?
    - What is the agreed-upon value of all the noncash contributions?
    - Are there contingencies to the contributions? (For example, maybe one partner is going to invest at the time of formation, while another partner is going to contribute capital over time.)
    - What happens if a partner can't contribute the agreed-upon money at the designated time?
    - If you want to be fifty-fifty partners, how is the partner contributing less equity going to pay back

the partner contributing more equity to equalize the contributions?
- Expectations for business operations
    - What is expected of each member throughout the term of the business?
    - If a partner is contributing services, how much time are they expected to spend?
    - What is considered a business expense? Is there a cap to these expenses? (Pay special attention to gray-area expenses such as marketing, meals, and entertainment.)
    - How will you equalize expenses when one partner spends more than another? (For example, maybe you agree that cell phone bills are a covered expense, but one member has his kids on his plan, so his cell phone bill is $450 a month, compared to another member's $100 cell phone bill. Will the partner with the lower bill get an additional $350 a month back in profit?)
- Long-term plan
    - How will profits be allocated?
    - What's the exit strategy?

BEST PRACTICES: HOW TO CHOOSE AN ENTITY STRUCTURE

There are several different questions you want to consider when choosing an entity structure.

- What's your exit strategy? Are you planning to sell soon?
- Which structure will give you the most tax benefits?
- What size is your business? If you plan to have shareholders, how many?
- Where will you be operating? Does your state have any rules or regulations regarding different entity structures? Does it require a certain entity structure for you to be able to get the business license(s) you need?
- How will profits be shared?
- Do you need to be protected from legal liabilities?

Your answers to these questions will all factor into your entity-structure choice.

EXIT STRATEGY

You should start a business with the end in mind. What is your exit strategy? Do you want to one day take your company public? Do you plan on establishing a strong foundation for your business and then passing it down to your children? Do you want to ramp up the business quickly and then sell it? Your chosen exit strategy will affect the entity structure you choose.

If you plan to sell your business soon, a C corporation or partnership structure could be beneficial, as these businesses are the easiest to sell, while sole proprietorships and S corporations are the most difficult to sell. However, if you're planning on passing the business down to someone else, an S corporation structure could be a good choice, as S corporations are great "lifestyle businesses," where you plan to operate the business indefinitely and use distributions from the business to fund your personal lifestyle.

TAXES

As already discussed in chapter 1, "Blaming Uncle Sam," there are a number of tax considerations to keep in mind when choosing your entity structure. Among the most important things to remember are that S corporations, sole proprietorships, and partnerships are flow-through entities, meaning the business's income is passed through and treated as your personal income.

C corporations are not flow-through entities, and so they are subject to double taxation. Recently, the C corporation tax rate was reduced, so this double taxation is not as much of an issue as it was in the past, although it is still a major consideration. If you're not in the highest income tax bracket, then generally speaking, you're going to get the best advantage from an S corporation over a C corporation. But if you have a lot of R&D credits you can take, you're better off as a C corporation.

Another major tax factor is that in sole proprietorships and partnerships, all the business's profit will be counted as your personal income and subject to self-employment taxes, meaning you'll have to pay all the Social Security and Medicare taxes on it. With an S corporation or C corporation, on the other hand, you have the option to reinvest the business's earnings into the business. You can also classify yourself as an employee and set yourself a normal salary. Any profits can then be distributed to you free of self-employment tax. For C corporations, though, because of the double taxation, shareholders are subject to dividend tax rates on any distributions of earnings and profits.

BUSINESS SIZE

If your business is just you, then a sole proprietorship (set up as an LLC for legal considerations I will get to in a moment) makes sense. Similarly, if your business is just you and one or a few other partners, then a partnership (set up as a multiple-member LLC) is likely a good idea.

If your business is substantial, with multiple employees and gross yearly profit of $100,000 or more, you will likely want to structure as a corporation. The major reason is the tax benefit mentioned above, where you can choose to invest part of the business's profit back into the business and not pay self-employment tax on it.

For small businesses not related to real estate ventures (which work well in partnerships), an S corporation ends up being the best choice, because of the ability to avoid the double taxation of a C corporation. However, S corporations are limited to having no more than one hundred shareholders. So if you want or expect to have more than that, a C corporation is the best choice for you. Most very large companies, such as *Fortune* 500 companies, are C corporations.

LOCATION

From state to state, the laws are slightly different for the various entity structures, and the tax rates also change.

For example, in Arizona, if you have an LLC, you pay no extra state taxes, but in California, you have to pay a minimum yearly franchise tax of $800 for the privilege to do business there.

If you want to operate in multiple states, you need to pay extra attention to the various requirements of each location. If you want to operate in Arizona, California, and Utah, it might be better for you to create three separate businesses, one for each state, with one master holding company that owns all three. Or maybe for your specific situation, it would be most advantageous to operate an LLC in California that does business in the other two states.

Different states also have different rules regarding what entity structure you're allowed to have. For example, if you have a small property management company, a single-member or multiple-member LLC might work well for you in the state of Arizona, but California requires property management companies to be C corporations, not S corporations or LLCs. LLCs can own stock, though, so if you want to do business in California, you might want to create a new master LLC that owns the stock of the C corporation in California.

Before you start doing business in another state, you really need advice from a professional, someone familiar with all the impacts setting foot in that state will have for you, such as tax and licensing requirements. For example, you'll want to determine whether you have nexus in that other state—that is, do you have sufficient physical presence in that state such that you must collect and pay taxes on those sales? Say you are based in Arizona, and you sell services to someone in New York. If you don't have any employees, equipment, or property (leased or owned) in New York, then you don't have to collect New York sales tax or pay New York state business taxes on the income generated from your New York customers.

FLEXIBILITY OF PROFIT SHARING

If you organize as a corporation, profit sharing is based on how many shares a person owns in the corporation. So if your company has one hundred shares and you own fifty of them, you have to take 50% of the dividends that are paid out.

On the other hand, if you have an LLC, you have more flexibility in how profit is distributed. This is the main reason multiple-member LLCs are so commonly used for real estate, because real estate deals typically involve a money partner and a sweat partner. The money partner might own 100% of the equity, but each partner can still get paid 50% of the profit distributions, as the distributions do not have to follow the exact number of shares or units of the business.

LEGAL CONSIDERATIONS

Sole proprietorships and partnerships, if not set up as LLCs, come with higher legal liability for the business owner/partners. With these entity structures, you can be held personally responsible for the business's liabilities.

This doesn't mean you need to avoid these entity structures entirely if you're worried about liability risk. Simply set your business up as a single-member or multiple-member LLC. When you set your business up as an LLC, you get liability protection while still being taxed as a sole proprietorship or partnership. When you have a multiple-member LLC, you are also shielded from liability for the actions of your partner(s).

In many states, LLCs are subject to additional fees and taxes compared to sole proprietorships and partnerships, but unless you have low to zero liability risk, the extra cost is worth the protection an LLC affords.

S corporations and C corporations come with legal liability protection already, so no need to take additional legal steps if you deem one of these structures best for your purposes.

If you get sued, there are different laws that come into play depending on your entity structure, but both LLCs and corporations have limited liability.

WHICH ENTITY STRUCTURE IS RIGHT FOR YOU?
Single-Member LLC/Sole Proprietorship

A single-member LLC (taxed as a sole proprietorship) is best if you have few or no employees and if the business's income is low enough that it makes sense for you to be paying self-employment tax on all of it. Single-member LLCs work well for freelancers and consultants, for example, where the business's profits are mostly equivalent to a year's salary.

Multiple-Member LLC/Partnership

If you have one or more partners and want to distribute profit based on something other than equity shares, a multiple-member LLC is likely an appropriate option for you. Multiple-member LLCs are the preferred entity structure for real estate businesses in particular.

S Corporation

Most small businesses do well as S corporations, especially if the business owner plans on living off the proceeds of the business and does not plan on selling the business. For example, most attorneys, accountants, and doctors are probably not going to switch professions anytime soon, so it makes sense for their businesses to be set up as S corporations. An S corporation might be the best choice for you if

- you're a smaller business, with fewer than one hundred shareholders;
- you're not in the highest income tax bracket;
- you're not planning on selling the business soon; and
- you don't plan to take advantage of R&D credits.

C Corporation

Most large businesses are structured as C corporations. A C corporation might be the best choice for you if

- you expect to have more than one hundred shareholders or want to offer different classes of stock;
- you plan to reinvest most of the proceeds of the business back into the business;
- you're planning on selling the business soon;
- you want to take advantage of R&D credits; and
- you are in the highest income tax bracket (meaning the double taxation of the C corporation won't affect you as much).

EQUITY CONSIDERATIONS IN A PARTNERSHIP
LIFESTYLE CONFLICTS

Different people have different lifestyles. If one partner is used to a certain standard of living and another is used to living more frugally, it is easy for conflicts to arise. That's why it is so important for you to define up front what is and is not acceptable in terms of the business. If you set out clear boundary lines in the beginning via an operating agreement, then you will have something to go back to and enforce if conflicts occur.

DECISIONS AMONG MULTIPLE PARTIES

In a partnership, you need to appoint one person to manage the business. Partners need to discuss and decide the big decisions together, but if you're trying to get five people to come to a consensus on what kind of paper to order for the office, you're never going to get anything done. Also, just think of it from a practical perspective of doing business. If you don't appoint one person as a manager, you'll all have to go in and open a bank account together, and every time there's a contract to be signed, you'll have to gather everyone's signatures. You need to appoint someone. There's a reason we have presidents and CEOs.

Have a manager who takes care of the day-to-day business operations. Set a dollar amount that this person can spend, and then for anything over that, all the partners can vote. The partners can also vote on any bigger-picture modifications to the business's vision and mission, culture, sales, or critical business processes.

EQUITY CONSIDERATIONS IN A CORPORATION
PROFIT SHARING

Profit sharing has to be pro rata in a corporation based on the number of shares a person holds. Define what each person is contributing to the business and then assign shares accordingly, understanding that a person's number of shares affects the amount of dividends they receive.

Set guidelines outlining at what point you will trigger a distribution of earnings. Essentially, what does your established reserve have to be before you start distributing money?

CONTRIBUTIONS OF CASH VERSUS EFFORT

For all shareholders, you need to define what they're going to invest, what they're expected to do, and what their expected return is. Also, outline relevant time periods, such as how soon a money partner can expect a return or how long a sweat partner is agreeing to contribute work to the company. Also, determine who has voting rights or nonvoting rights in the corporation. Establishing all these things in the beginning will prevent disputes later on.

Money partners want an ROI in a reasonable amount of time, because they're putting up all the money to make the business happen. As a result, you may need to specify a guaranteed ROI that will be realized within a set amount of time.

Sweat partners in a corporation are typically considered employees of the corporation and not shareholders. Usually, the only way for them to get shares is to pay taxes on wage income and contribute that net to the business to buy shares.

In addition, unlike money partners, sweat partners are

typically not guaranteed a certain return on their investment. Instead, their return is based on the success of the business. In real estate flipping, for example, if a property sells for less than expected, the money partner may still receive their guaranteed return, while the sweat partner's return will take a direct hit. Sweat partners do not always have the ability to choose their income level, because their returns depend directly on how much profit the business turns. As such, they must be prepared for variability in their income, including potential lean times.

KEY TIPS

- **Be careful what you sign.** You always need to really look at what you're signing, from operating agreements to vendor contracts. You get busy. I understand—I get busy too. When you have a million other things on your mind, it's easier to just sign those things that appear to be boilerplate or have a lot of fine print. Despite the temptation, really review everything you sign so that you understand what you're committing to. Otherwise, you might run into issues later on. For example, I once had a client whose operating agreement had clearly been copied and pasted from another business. On the surface, everything looked professional and in order, but once you actually started reading it, you realized there were a lot of issues, including blatant inaccuracies, such as references to partners who did not exist. If there are any sections you don't understand while reviewing a contract, highlight them and contact an attorney.

- **Watch out for tax consequences.** Make sure you're not taking advances on your distributions so that you don't inadvertently make a sale of equity and get a tax surprise.
- **Determine what you are willing to commit.** More than any other factor, the success of your business depends on you and what you are willing to commit, both in terms of money and effort. Many people sink all the money they have into their business. Sometimes it pays off, and sometimes it doesn't. Are you investing your life savings? Did you withdraw all your retirement plan money? How far are you willing to go? It's important to determine how much you are willing to invest and thus how much you are willing to lose. If you don't set guidelines at the beginning, it is easy to fall into the sunk-cost fallacy, where the more you invest into something, the harder it becomes to abandon it. You need to determine an amount of money that you are comfortable investing. Just as important as the money you're willing to invest is the time and sweat you're willing to invest. What is it going to take to get to your first dollar of income? Will you go above and beyond to make your business work? No one else is going to do it except you. When you start a business, you want to get a skilled team in place fairly quickly,

but there is no guarantee you'll get the people you need, and so the work will fall to you. Being a business owner is *hard*. I can't even count the number of late nights I've spent at the office or the times I've had to go without paychecks. The market is not guaranteed. There will be ups and downs. If you don't have a strong commitment, when times get tough, your business won't survive.

- **Be prepared to live frugally.** As an entrepreneur, you have to be willing to sometimes go without—go without sleep, go without time, and go without money. You're not guaranteed a regular paycheck, so you must know how frugally you can live. You may have to go through weeks or even months where money is incredibly tight. Be prepared to go without certain luxuries.
- **Have a good accounting system.** Have I said this enough yet? If you don't have a dependable accounting system, you can't track the results of your business. A business without an accounting system is like a student without a report card. Without a report card, you have no way of knowing how your child is doing in school. Are they failing any classes? Are they struggling in any particular subject? Your accounting system will give you a report card for your business. Your accounting system can also help you keep track of who put what equity into the business and how much each shareholder member should receive in dividends.

CHAPTER 11

GETTING PAID

WHAT IS YOUR REVENUE?

After going through the balance sheet for your business, you can begin looking at the profit and loss (P&L) statement. The first category to look at on the P&L is revenue/income. Here is what that part of the P&L might look like for a service company:

Excerpt Service Income

	Jan–Dec 2017	Jan–Dec 2016	Change
Income			
CFO Services	1,082,145	279,475	802,670
Accounting Services	124,968	16,190	108,777
Retirement Plan Administration	12,181	3,939	8,242
Payroll Services	205,912	226,758	(20,846)
Tax Services	298,355	724,910	(426,555)
Consulting Services	102,808	175,896	(73,089)
Tax Controversy Services	24,130	8,360	15,770
Finance Charges	289	123	166
Discounts & Allowances	(1,790)	(106,804)	105,014
Total Income	**1,848,997**	**1,328,848**	**520,149**

And here's an example of what it might look like for a retail company:

Excerpt Cannabis Income

	Corporate	Branch 1	Branch 2	Branch 3	TOTAL
Income					
Consulting Income	600,000		-		600,000
Sales		2,900,477	3,752,621	716,982	7,370,080
Cash Over/(Short)		26,462	(4,133)	241	22,570
Gratuities			110		110
Refunds		(180)	(25)		(205)
Total Income	**600,000**	**2,926,759**	**3,748,573**	**717,223**	**7,992,555**

THE IMPORTANCE OF TRACKING REVENUE—FIGURING OUT PROFITABILITY

John felt as if his computer company was making a profit, but he never had any cash, so he contacted eeCPA for help. John brought in all the financial statements his bookkeeper had pulled for him, and the P&L was five pages long. Five pages! No wonder John didn't have a grip on how much profit his business was actually making. I can't stress it enough: simpler is easier for everyone and will help you spot problem areas and red flags.

John's P&L contained dozens of different income lines. There was a whole page dedicated just to the income portion of the P&L when the entire P&L should be only one or two pages. Because there were so many different income streams listed, it was impossible to determine which services were profitable.

There were also many redundant services. For example, the company offered some white-label services (services they sold to other companies, who rebranded them as their own). They spent a lot of time separating each white-label service from the normal-service equivalent in their financial system, essentially doubling their services. In reality, the services were one and the same; the cost of providing the services was the same and the sale price was similar, so there was no reason to separate them on the P&L.

We were able to categorize all their different services into three main categories: tech-support contracts, backup services (which they outsourced), and custom programming services. From there, we drilled down a little further, as they sold to both individuals and businesses and had different pricing for the two. So in the end, we whittled their page of income streams down to just three lines of revenue categories, broken into two further categories each. Here's an example of how that looked:

Income by Class

	Residential	Commercial	Total
	Income		
Tech Support	1,000,000	500,000	1,500,000
Backup Services	200,000	500,000	700,000
Custom Programming	250,000	750,000	1,000,000
Total Income	1,450,000	1,750,000	3,200,000

Pretty clear, right?

With this new setup, we were able to clearly link the revenue different services brought in with the cost of producing those services. We then discovered that although custom programming was generating $1 million in revenue, the cost of producing that revenue was $1.2 million. So John was losing $200,000 on this type of service. The custom programming helped drive support-service sales, but they weren't making enough on the support services to justify the $200,000 loss. So obviously, they had to either change something or stop offering the programming service.

REVENUE

TOP-LINE REVENUE

Top-line revenue is your sales—all the income you bring in before accounting for expenses. Top-line revenue is what your point-of-sale system will show. Remember, though, that a sales order is not revenue. Your top-line revenue should include only the sales that have actually been completed.

GROSS PROFIT

Gross profit is your top-line revenue minus the direct costs of producing your service or product.

In the next chapter, I'll go into detail on what qualifies as a direct cost, but in general, if you're selling a product, then the cost to manufacture that product is your direct cost, and if you're selling a service, then the cost of labor to produce that service is your direct cost.

COMMON MISCONCEPTIONS ABOUT REVENUE

MYTH #1: A SALES ORDER IS A SALE

I've touched on this idea briefly already. Many people think a sales order is a sale, but a sales order is an order, not a sale. You've received the order from the customer, so you have a commitment to supply or fulfill the contract for your customer, but you don't recognize the revenue until you actually earn it. So if the order is for a product, until that product ships or reaches the customer, you haven't earned the revenue. It's the same with services. Until you fulfill the service requirements, the sale is not really complete.

A basic principle of accounting is that you need to match your revenue to your expenses. If you haven't fulfilled a sale yet, you haven't incurred the expenses. Until you incur those expenses and can thus match the expenses to the revenue, you can't count that revenue. You'll notice if you place an order with Amazon, they don't charge your card until they ship the item, even though you put all your credit card information in as soon as you make the purchase.

MYTH #2: A DEPOSIT IS A SALE

This myth goes hand in hand with the myth that a sales order is a sale. Only a completed sale is a sale. Even if you receive a partial or full deposit from a customer, that money isn't revenue until you fulfill the sale. That money needs to sit as a liability on your balance sheet, as it comes with an obligation, or liability, to provide the promised product or service. Then, once you fulfill the sale, you can move the money over to your P&L as revenue.

The reasoning behind this again goes back to matching revenue and expenses. Let's say you cater events and get a $5,000 deposit in February for a wedding in April. If you record the sale in February, you will be recognizing revenue in February, but the expenses won't hit until April, when the event occurs. You won't be able to determine the profitability of that event because your revenue and expenses are occurring in two different periods.

This issue commonly arises with gift cards. One of my clients owns a medical spa, and they frequently sell gift cards to their clients. The revenue from these gift cards must not be recorded when the gift card is sold but either when the client uses the gift card (when the corresponding expenses are incurred) or when the gift card expires (in which case no corresponding expenses are a possibility and you get free, easy profit). Until a gift card is either used or expires, it should be listed as a liability on the balance sheet.

Part of the problem with how deposits and the like are recorded is that a lot of people use QuickBooks or similar software, and it's not very intuitive how to correctly record deposits in such software. At eeCPA, our solution is to create a nonposting sales order that invoices the customer. So the customer still receives an invoice to pay against, but the system doesn't record a receivable and thus doesn't record revenue. The money the customer pays sits on their account as a credit. Once the sale is fulfilled, the credit on the account is used up and classified as revenue. At the end of each month, we go through the accounts. If a sale hasn't been fulfilled, then a credit will still be sitting on the account, and we know to classify this amount as a liability.

By using this method, the cash amount is correct because the business did receive and cash the deposit, but the money is not listed as revenue on their P&L, as it should not be. This method also allows the business to clearly see their outstanding liabilities related to sale fulfillment.

It is important to properly classify deposits and gift cards as liabilities, because if you don't, then when it comes time to fulfill the sale, you might not have the resources available to do so.

MYTH #3: ALL REVENUE IS COLLECTIBLE

Again, as mentioned previously, not all revenue is always collectible. You might have made a sale, but if you can't get paid on the sale, then it's not really a sale. This is why it is so important for you to implement good accounts receivable policies, as outlined in chapter 8.

WHAT YOU NEED TO KNOW ABOUT REVENUE

NONREFUNDABLE DEPOSITS

If you accept nonrefundable deposits and are using the cash method of accounting, then for tax purposes, those deposits have to be recognized as income. However, from a financial perspective, even nonrefundable deposits are still deposits and should be listed as liabilities until the sale is fulfilled or until the customer has backed out of the sale and you've determined that no work is going to be performed (and thus no expenses will be incurred). At that point, you can post the deposit as income.

RECORDING REVENUE BEFORE SALE IS COMPLETED = CHASING REVENUE

The people who record revenue before completing the sale tend to be the people who chase revenue. They think that the higher the revenue, the better their business is doing. Revenue does not matter nearly as much as profit, though. So instead of falsely boosting your revenue numbers by recording revenue before a sale is completed, match your revenue with expenses so that you can get an accurate picture of your profit.

Recording revenue before the sale is completed will also put you in the position of chasing after the actual money associated with that sale. Because your financial statements say you have the revenue, you will make your decisions accordingly, and then you'll have to put in extra effort to make sure that the sale doesn't fall through and that the customer actually pays you.

FALSE SENSE OF PROFIT

Recording revenue before a sale is completed can make it appear that you're much more profitable than you really are, because you haven't incurred any of the expenses of the sale yet.

Let's go back to the example of the wedding caterer. If they record the $5,000 deposit they receive in February as revenue, then they will have an extra $5,000 going straight into their gross profit, as they haven't had to purchase any of the food supplies or pay for any of the labor that will be required when the wedding occurs, in April. Because it looks like that $5,000 is profit, they might end up spending that money on something else. Then a few months later, when they have to shell out $5,000 for the expenses for that wedding, they might have to stretch to make ends meet. Plus, their gross profit for that month is going to take a direct hit, as they're incurring lots of expenses while not bringing in the full amount of corresponding revenue.

Also remember that if you're on the cash method of accounting, recording deposits in this way can result in increased taxes for you if your total profit appears higher than it really is.

COST INCREASES BETWEEN THE TIME OF DEPOSIT AND DELIVERY

You might think, *If all that matters is matching revenue and expenses, why can't I just record my expected expenses so that I can get a deposit on the books as revenue right away?* The issue is that estimated costs aren't good enough. The costs associated with a sale could easily increase between receipt of the deposit and delivery of the product or service, impacting your profit. To have true profit numbers, you have to record the *actual* costs, not projected costs.

Say you quoted a paint job to a customer in December 2016, with the labor cost based on minimum wage—$8.50 an hour. Your customer agreed to the quote and gave you the deposit in December for the work to be completed in February. Well, when January 1, 2017, rolled around, the minimum wage went up to $10 an hour, making your labor cost $1.50 more per hour. If originally you had planned to make $5 an hour of profit, now you are set to make only $3.50 of profit an hour—30% less than planned.

BEST PRACTICES: HOW TO TRACK REVENUE
LIMIT NUMBER OF SERVICES/PRODUCTS

Less is more when it comes to your P&L. You want a simple, big-picture overview of your business. This way, you can easily identify your business's strengths and weaknesses. You can always dive down into details later.

For service companies, shoot for having no more than twelve different types of service on the revenue section of your P&L. You can group services based on different price points or based on different types of activity. In the example from the start of the chapter with the computer company, we did both. We grouped based on three different types of activity (tech-support contracts, backup services, and custom programming services) and based on two different price points (individuals vs. businesses).

For retail companies, group products into as few categories as possible.

If you sell both wholesale and retail, it makes a lot of sense to list those as separate categories. Wholesale is generally sold at a lower margin than retail, but there is often a higher cost of doing business in retail. So it is important to separate out the two revenue streams, match them to direct costs, and then calculate out the profit margins of each to see which direction you want to take your business.

If you have multiple branches at your business, you could separate by branch to see the profit margin each location is achieving.

Or if you sell on different platforms—maybe you have your own online store, sell on a third-party website such as Etsy or Amazon, and also have a brick-and-mortar store—categorizing revenue by those platforms could provide useful information.

There are a lot of different ways to categorize your revenue streams. If you're uncertain about what is best for your business, consult an expert.

DETERMINE PROFITABILITY OF EACH SERVICE/PRODUCT

The overall goal here is to determine the profitability of each service or product you offer. The best way to do this is to categorize your revenue in alignment with direct cost. That means matching a service or product with a corresponding cost of goods sold line on your P&L. You don't necessarily need to have a matching cost of goods line for *every* revenue stream, but you want to have a matching line for all the biggest revenue streams. In this way, you can define your most profitable line of revenue, and then you can focus attention there.

In the restaurant business, food has a different gross profit margin than beverages. Alcohol and soda are generally far more profitable than food, due to the higher costs of the food as well as all the higher labor costs associated with preparing the food. Maybe you determine that you're not making enough profit in your restaurant, so you decide to raise all your food prices by 20%. This is a pretty significant increase, so you might lose some customers as a result. However, maybe instead you could raise just your beverage prices 10% and increase your bottom line the same amount, as beverages have such a high profit margin. With just a 10% increase on drinks only, you're less likely to lose many customers.

Or to go back to the tech company example, maybe John makes a 50% gross profit on commercial tech-support services ($500,000 revenue) and only a 20% profit on residential tech-support services ($1 million in revenue). He may decide to keep the residential services because he needs the cash flow, but he can start marketing the commercial division more heavily because he knows he can make a much higher profit margin on those services. Or he can make changes to increase the residential services' profit margin, such as revamping the training program in order to reduce support-call times by ten minutes apiece.

If you don't separate your revenue into a few key categories and then match those revenue streams to their respective costs, you won't even get to the place where you can make these kinds of strategic decisions about your business. Once you figure out the profitability of your different types of income, then you can tweak things.

KEY TIPS

- **Align deposits/revenue with fulfillment of the sale.** Follow the matching principle of accounting—match income with expenses so that you can determine your gross profit margin.
- **Have a clear idea of the profit margin for each revenue type.** Even if your business is turning a respectable profit overall, you might have certain products or services that aren't earning you as much as they should be or might even be costing you money. Figure out the profit margin of each type of revenue so that you can make adjustments where needed.
- **Limit the number of revenue categories.** You always want to make decisions based on valid information, and when you keep it simple, your information is more likely to be accurate. If you have fifty different types of revenue, transactions are bound to be miscat-

egorized at some point. With fewer categories, there will be fewer mistakes. Incorrect information won't help you run your business, so keep it simple and easy.

CHAPTER 12

BREAKING EVEN

WHAT ARE YOUR DIRECT COSTS?

The next part of your P&L after revenue is direct costs, or costs of goods sold. Here's an example of what that might look like for a service company:

Excerpt Service Direct Costs

	Jan–Dec 2017	Jan–Dec 2016	Change
Direct Client Costs			
Client Expenses	59,568	3,850	55,718
Client Service Guarantee	1,126	-	1,126
Total Direct Client Costs	60,694	3,850	56,844

And here's an example of what it might look like for a retail company:

Excerpt Cannabis Direct Cost

	Corporate	Branch 1	Branch 2	Branch 3	TOTAL
		Cost of Goods Sold			
Medical Director		9,000	11,000	3,000	23,000
Security Guards/Alarm	13,100	136,615	341,828	63,177	554,719
Total Applied Overhead	13,100	145,615	352,828	66,177	577,719
Cost of Goods Sold		1,720,669	1,927,291	650,299	4,298,259
Supplies			-	1,320	1,320
Total Direct Costs	-	1,720,669	1,927,291	651,619	4,299,579
Total Cost of Goods Sold	**13,100**	**1,866,283**	**2,280,119**	**717,796**	**4,877,298**

PROFIT OR LOSS—FACTORING IN DIRECT COSTS

One of my clients sells travel memberships, and as an ancillary benefit for their customers, they run an online store where members can buy wine at a discounted rate. They never intended to make a profit on these wine sales, as this perk is simply a way to drive sales of travel memberships—their main business. They just wanted to break even.

The wine they were selling cost $15 a bottle, so they priced it online at $30, with members being able to redeem points to bring the price down to $15. They thought they were selling at cost at $15 and would break even. They were wrong.

Unfortunately, when they set the pricing, they forgot to include the cost of packing and shipping. A lot goes into shipping a bottle of wine across the country. The wine has to be packed carefully to prevent it from breaking; as alcohol, it needs special labeling; and its temperature has to stay consistent. All told, packing and shipping costs added an additional $25 per bottle.

So their real cost for each bottle was $40, not $15. Even when customers didn't redeem points and bought the wine at $30, the company was losing $10. When customers did redeem points, the company was losing a whopping $25 a bottle.

When calculating price points, you have to be careful to factor in all direct costs of fulfilling the sale. In nearly all cases, if your gross profit margin is negative, you're going to have an unsustainable business. The only exception to this is loss leaders, where you offer a service or sell an item at a loss in order to attract customers. For example, a grocery store might offer six-packs of Coke for a dollar just to get people into the store. The store takes a loss on the Coke, but once people are there, they spend a hundred bucks on other things, and so the grocery store makes up for the loss.

In this company's case, while the wine was never meant to be profitable, it definitely wasn't meant to be a loss leader either. We informed the wine client of the loss and recommended that they either add on a shipping fee, price the bottle at $80 and then discount it down to $40, or figure out a way to reduce the direct costs so that they would break even. They decided to increase prices and began selling only half cases or full cases instead of individual bottles, thus reducing their shipping costs. With these changes, they were able to break even.

DIRECT COSTS

Direct costs are all the expenses that drive revenue—all the costs directly associated with a sale. So all the costs for labor and materials that go into fulfilling a sale are direct costs. A good way to think of it is that direct costs are the costs that wouldn't be there if you didn't make a sale.

Direct costs also include all the costs related to supporting the customer, such as software licenses, filing fees, client expenses (all the miscellaneous expenses incurred for the client, such as travel expenses, courier delivery charges, or professional consultant costs), and service guarantees.

I'll use eeCPA as an example. In addition to providing our various services, we sell QuickBooks software licenses to our clients. The cost of those licenses is a direct cost because we only have to pay for those licenses if we sell them. On the other hand, all the software licenses and apps we pay for just to be in business are *not* direct costs. They are overhead costs—costs we would be paying even if we did not make any sales.

In addition to the cost of the software licenses we sell, we have various filing fees and client expenses we must pay, such as the fees to organize a new entity or the costs to hire professional consultants. We also offer a service guarantee. All of these costs are incurred in relation to our sales. If we didn't make a sale, we wouldn't have to pay the filing fees or hire support labor or fulfill our service guarantee. So these costs are all direct costs.

At eeCPA, we sell our services as packages. We're not selling just software licenses or just filing fees. Because of this, there is no reason for us to separate our direct costs out into software licenses, filing fees, and so on. Instead, we group all the costs into the one category of "client expenses"—all the expenses we incur in providing our service. If we didn't have the client, then we wouldn't have these expenses.

Similar to why your everyday-use software and apps are

not considered direct costs, payroll costs are also calculated separately from direct costs. You've committed to having those people work full time or part time, and you have to pay their salaries regardless of whether you make sales. If you've hired a receptionist to answer the phones from 9:00 a.m. to 5:00 p.m. and no calls come in one day, you're still paying her for eight hours of work.

On the other hand, sometimes you might hire someone directly in relation to a sale. Maybe you hire a consultant for a month to oversee the rollout of a custom product line your top client has ordered, or maybe you hire a subcontractor to do all the painting on a particular construction project. In that case, those labor costs should be categorized as direct costs, as you wouldn't have hired those people and incurred those expenses if you hadn't made the sale.

COMMON MISCONCEPTIONS ABOUT DIRECT COSTS

MYTH #1: VARIABLE COSTS ARE DIRECT COSTS AND FIXED COSTS ARE INDIRECT COSTS

Yes, in general, direct costs tend to be variable, and indirect costs tend to be fixed. However, the terms are not interchangeable.

Variable costs are those costs that change in proportion

based on output. With variable costs, the more you sell, the more your costs are. So raw materials are a variable cost because the more you sell, the more raw materials you have to buy in order to fulfill those sales.

Fixed costs do not change regardless of how output changes. Sales can go up or down, and your fixed costs will remain the same. Rent is a great example of a fixed cost because it remains the same regardless of how much you produce.

Although generally direct costs are variable and indirect costs are fixed, direct costs can be fixed and indirect costs can be variable.

In the previous example of hiring a consultant to oversee the rollout of a new custom product line, that person's wages are a direct but fixed cost. That person was hired specifically in relation to the sale of that new product, but the amount that person is paid isn't going to change based on how many products are produced.

In some cases, utilities are an example of a variable indirect cost. If your business relies on equipment that uses electricity, then when you're producing more, you're using that equipment more and using more electricity. Thus, your electricity usage is a variable indirect cost. Note, however, that we're not talking about the utilities for lights in your office or air-conditioning—those things would be indirect costs, as you're using them regardless of whether you make the sale. We're also not talking about your utilities going up based on the season. In that case, the change is based on weather, and variable costs are only when the change is based on production output.

For the vast majority of cases, your direct costs will be variable and your indirect costs will be fixed, but it is still best to understand the unique meanings of the terms.

MYTH #2: YOU NEED TO ALLOCATE ALL YOUR COSTS

For companies that make $5 million or less in revenue, allocating all the costs is simply not feasible. It takes a full team of financial professionals to be able to allocate all the costs, both direct and indirect. If your business is pulling in less than $5 million a year, focus only on direct costs, and keep the number of cost categories limited. Identify your largest revenue streams, and separate the direct costs into a matching number of categories so that you can determine the profitability of those revenue streams. Remember that you can always drill deeper in specific categories as needed.

Once you hit that $5 million yearly revenue point, then you can invest the time and money into allocating and analyzing all the costs so that you can refine your business for scaling purposes. If you're faced with a particular business decision, such as whether to hire a new employee, you can also choose to allocate certain subsets of costs to get information that will help you make that decision. You could even allocate costs by employee to measure productivity. But for your big-picture P&L, you want only the overview, and allocating all the costs would just serve to clutter the statement.

Let's say you own a pest control company making less than $5 million in revenue. You have ten field service workers as well as two in-office customer support agents. The field service workers are paid per job, while the in-office customer support agents are paid hourly at $15 an hour. We'll say each job costs $100, and the field service workers get $25 per job and complete about ten jobs per day on average. The in-office customer support agents' salaries, on the other hand, are indirect costs.

So total, you're bringing in $10,000 in revenue a day (ten field service workers with ten jobs apiece at $100 a pop). Because the field service workers are paid per job, their wages are a direct cost (really, everything associated with paying them, including taxes, benefits, and so on, would be considered a direct cost, but for simplicity's sake, we're going to use just wages in this example). That cost comes out to $2,500 (ten field service workers, each with ten jobs, being paid $25 per job). The in-office customer support agents' salaries, on the other hand, are indirect costs. You could go ahead and allocate that indirect cost out, but the in-office customer support agents' daily wages comes out to just $240 (again, for simplicity's sake, we're not factoring in all the associated payroll costs beyond wage, but these extra costs would be included in a full analysis).

Plus, that cost is fixed. If you didn't make any service calls one day for some reason—maybe due to weather—and you allocated the indirect cost of the in-office customer support, the service would seem incredibly unprofitable, as it was costing money while not bringing in any revenue. If you want to know the profitability of the service, it makes more sense to look at the much higher and direct cost of the field-service workers' salary.

MYTH #3: YOU ONLY HAVE TO WORRY ABOUT HIRING TOO MANY PEOPLE, NOT HIRING TOO FEW

Obviously, if you hire too many people, you will be stuck paying unnecessary wages, lowering your profit margin. However, when you factor in overtime and loss of revenue, hiring too few people can be just as much of a problem as hiring too many people.

Let's use the pest control company example again. This

time, let's say the field service workers are paid hourly, at $30 an hour, not by job. So in a normal eight-hour day, they make $240. We'll say they're still doing ten jobs a day at $100 a job, bringing in $1,000 in revenue. So after subtracting their daily wages (for ease, we're not worrying about any other direct costs right now), you make $760 in profit each day. That means your profit margin is 76%. With ten service workers, that's a total profit of $7,600.

Right now, maybe there's more work than can be fit into an eight-hour day, so your field service workers regularly work ten hours, doing twelve jobs a day. So now their total wages are $240 for the first eight hours, plus the overtime rate of $45 for two hours, bringing the total daily wage to $330. Each of them is bringing in $1,200 in revenue now, so your total profit per service worker is $870, with a profit margin of 72.5%. With ten service workers, that's a total profit of $8,700.

Each of your guys is doing two extra jobs a day, though. That's a total of twenty extra jobs among all of them, so really, let's say you could hire two new field service workers instead. Now you're bringing in $12,000 in revenue each day (twelve workers with ten jobs apiece at $100 a job). Because you're not paying overtime, you get the 76% profit margin, meaning $9,120. That's an extra $420 straight to your profit.

Pest Control Company: Gross Profit Analysis

	Hourly w/2 Hours of OT per Person	Hourly at Zero Overtime—Hire 2 Employees
Daily Sales	12,000	12,000
	Direct Costs	
Direct Labor	10	12
Quantity	8	8
Rate	30	30
Regular Wage Costs	2,400	2,880
Direct Labor	10	
Overtime Rate	45	
Overtime Hours	2	
Overtime Costs	900	
Total Daily Labor Cost	3,300	2,880
Gross Profit	8,700	9,120
	73%	76%

Now, in this example, I'm not factoring in all the ancillary payroll costs. Considering those extra costs, you probably wouldn't want to actually hire *two* new guys, but you get the idea.

You have to track the costs and do the math to make sure you're employing the right number of people, not too many and not too few.

SALES AND MARKETING

Sales commissions are a direct cost, but otherwise, sales and marketing is typically an overhead cost. Because sales and marketing accounts for a large number of expenses, separate it into its own category on the P&L.

Marketing is an expensive area for a business, so it needs to drive revenue and give an ROI. It should produce qualified leads, increase brand awareness, or move your business forward in some way.

It's easy to get carried away with marketing. Avoid the temptation to try several new strategies all at once. You can't always directly correlate marketing with sales perfectly, but you want to track the effectiveness of your marketing strategies to the best of your ability. It's easier to do this if you focus on just a couple of strategies at a time.

There are four main marketing costs associated with identifying and contacting potential clients: advertising, networking, promotions, and web presence.

Digital advertising is easy to track. If you use pay-per-click advertising, such as Google AdWords, you can get clear reports on the number of clicks and the number of resulting leads. You can then easily beta test different ads and assess their efficacy.

To track the effectiveness of your nondigital advertising, you can ask your customers how they heard about you, perhaps through a customer survey. In addition, if you launch one large advertising campaign at a time, you could look at your base sales numbers to see if there is a clear increase.

Networking and branding can be a bit harder to track, as sometimes the leads won't materialize for months. I might meet with ten people at an event, and then it could be six months before I generate any sales from that event. Even though it might take a while to see the results, keep a list of leads from such networking events, and keep track of how many convert to sales.

For promotions, you can keep track of how many people take advantage of a certain discount or sale. However, take this information with a grain of salt, as there is no way for you to know that the promotion is what brought them in the door. I might choose to go to Fry's grocery store instead of Safeway because Fry's has bread on sale that week. There's really no way for Fry's to know that it was the bread sale and not the sale on milk that made me come to them instead of Safeway, though.

For web presence, you can track the number of online sales as well as the number of website hits. You also want to track how many of those hits turn into qualified leads.

For eeCPA, we were getting a ton of hits on our website, but most of them were just people price shopping—not qualified leads. By tracking the conversion rate, we were able to recognize the problem and remarket ourselves online.

In addition to tracking the subcategories of marketing, you could also track the global per-lead marketing cost of your business. For example, one cannabis company I work with spends $15,000 a week in sales and marketing costs, and they're getting five hundred new patients a week. Only medical marijuana is allowed in Arizona, so once a person becomes a patient at a particular dispensary, it is likely they will be a long-term customer. So from a global perspective, $15,000 a week for five hundred new patients means the cannabis company is spending $30 per new patient. Considering that the average patient spends $100 per month, the $30 is a great investment for $1,200 in annual revenue.

That global number can be useful to know, but do still keep track of the effectiveness of the individual marketing strategies. I had one software client who had a pretty good global cost per client acquisition. But one of their biggest marketing costs was getting booths at various industry trade shows. They would spend $10,000 per trade show and get maybe one or two qualified leads out of it. For a long time, they insisted that they had to keep going, or else people would think they'd gone out of business. After years, I finally convinced them to shift to other marketing strategies—email marketing, direct calling, direct meetings, and webinars—and we were able to generate far more qualified leads at far less cost.

Your marketing costs should ideally be 5% of the resulting annual revenue that is generated and no more than 10%. At eeCPA, for example, we pay $2,500 each month on pay-per-click ads that result in ten qualified leads—so $250 per lead. Typically, we get $500 a month in revenue from a client, or $6,000 for the year. That puts our marketing cost for each lead ($250) at about 4% of the total annual revenue the lead brings in. That's a great ROI.

It is important to continue tracking the efficacy of your various marketing strategies, though. Just because these pay-per-click ads work for eeCPA right now doesn't mean they will still work well for us three years from now. If the ads ever begin to cost more than 10% of the resulting revenue, we will have to reassess and look for new strategies.

In addition to marketing costs, you also have to track the sales expenses of converting leads to paying clients. These costs include travel, meals, entertainment, and collateral materials, (e.g., brochures, business cards, and promotional merchandise such as branded pens, water bottles, etc.).

Here's an example of how the sales and marketing section might look on a P&L:

Excerpt Sales & Marketing

	Jan–Dec 2017	Jan–Dec 2016	Change
Sales & Marketing			
Advertising		563	(563)
Client Events	87	7,249	(7,162)
Client Rewards	332	5,771	(5,439)
Holiday	1,109	1,164	(55)
Marketing & Promotion	1,239	7,468	(6,229)
Meals & Entertainment	2,273	2,010	262
Networking	3,696	5,167	(1,470)
Printing and Reproduction	2,842	8,786	(5,944)
Public Relations	10,150		10,150
Referral Gifts	435	972	(537)
Sponsorship	3,959		3,959
Travel	10,281	6,996	3,285
Website	12,646	22,392	(9,746)
Total Sales & Marketing	**49,049**	**68,537**	**(19,488)**

BEST PRACTICES: HOW TO ACCOUNT FOR DIRECT AND INDIRECT COSTS

IDENTIFY THE COST OF FULFILLING THE SALE

Start by identifying all the costs of fulfilling the sale. Know what your largest costs are and put your efforts into managing them first.

SET PRICING TO ACCOMMODATE A 10%–15% SHIFT IN COSTS

You never know when your direct costs might increase unexpectedly, so you want to build a buffer into your profit margin.

For example, at eeCPA, we use a lot of Intuit products, and in September 2017, we received notice that they would be raising prices 20% in thirty days, starting in October. Most of our client contracts renew in January, so we were already locked into prices with most of our customers. That meant we would be the ones to eat the price increase in October, November, and December. Luckily, we always include a price buffer in our sales contracts, so we were able to absorb that increase without losing money, but this increase did reduce our profit by 20% for the three months. Then in January, we revised our pricing structure to account for the increase and passed that extra cost on to the customer.

TRACK COSTS AGAINST REVENUE AND TRACK BASELINE GROSS PROFIT MARGIN PERCENTAGE

As discussed in the previous chapter, you always want to be sure to match revenue and expenses so that you can accurately track profitability. In addition, you should have a goal gross profit margin in mind and should track the percentage from month to month. Anytime your gross profit margin percentage drops too low, you should reevaluate your costs and their efficacy in driving revenue.

A large part of accurately tracking costs against revenue is recording prepaid expenses appropriately. For example, let's say you're going to a trade show. Maybe you pay for your booth at the show in January, the airline tickets in March, and then the hotel and food costs in June, when the trade show occurs. With the expenses all spread out, it can be difficult to assess the true total cost of going to the trade show.

When expenses are paid ahead of time, they should be listed on the balance sheet as an asset of prepaid expenses. Then, once you actually go to the trade show, they can be moved over to your P&L as expenses. Then you can accurately see the full cost of the trade show and assess its cost benefit as a marketing strategy.

ADJUST ACCORDING TO CHANGES IN THE MARKETPLACE

You want to be nimble and quick in response to market changes. If a competitor lowers prices, you will have to see if you can adjust to make a profit at that price point too. If you can't, then maybe you need to change your sales methodology or scrap that product or service entirely and focus your attention elsewhere. Or if a competitor raises prices, maybe you can raise prices, too, and increase your profit margin.

NEGOTIATE FIRM PRICING WITH VENDORS AND ALIGN CUSTOMER AND VENDOR CONTRACT RENEWALS

Negotiate contracts with your vendors in a way that guarantees you certain prices so you won't be surprised by increases. Also, be aware of when your contracts come up for renewal. Try to align your customer contract renewals with your vendor renewals so that if there are price increases, you can adjust your own prices accordingly and pass the increase on to your customers. Otherwise, you could be stuck eating a loss for months before you can raise your own prices.

Sometimes getting the right vendor contract is even more important than your customer contracts. Your vendor contracts determine a huge portion of your direct costs, so spend the time to negotiate the best terms you can.

FIND CREATIVE SOLUTIONS TO COST INCREASES

Sometimes raising your own prices isn't enough to offset a price increase, so you have to be prepared to look for other solutions. You may wish to shift your focus entirely, or maybe you can find new ways to increase efficiency.

Or maybe, as was the case for my client Harry, you can produce the item you need yourself.

Harry produces a natural thyroid medicine, and the main ingredient he needs to make this medicine is pig thyroid. Previously, there was only one main processor of pig thyroids in the country. Harry had been dealing with this company for many years and had a long-term contract at a fixed price—$700 per pound of thyroid powder.

With pig thyroids at this price, he was able to sell his product for $18 a bottle. Natural thyroid medicine is a niche product, so he had only two other competitors selling similar products. They sold their products for $44 and $62, so he was the clear winner when it came to price. Thanks in large part to the low cost of his medicine, he was making more than $20 million in revenue a year.

Then the business owner of the pig thyroid processor died, and his children took over the business. They raised the price of the pig thyroid 50%, to $1,050. Then the children wanted to sell the business, so they raised the price again, more than double this time, from $1,050 to $2,300 per pound.

That's a significant cost increase—more than triple what Harry had been paying before—so obviously, his gross profit margin went down quite a bit. Luckily, in addition to employing eeCPA for tax strategy, he also has a full-time controller and support staff. They always carefully watch the gross profit margin, so they were able to identify the issue immediately.

No matter how Harry tried to negotiate, the vendor refused to lower the price. So Harry was forced to buy for a while at the increased price. He didn't want to lose customers, so he refused to raise his own prices to help account for the increase. As a result, his bottom line took a significant hit. He was used to profit of upward of $10 million but pulled in only $6 million in 2017 as a result of the price increase.

Harry knew that he couldn't sustain his business with the higher pig thyroid cost. His business model was based on being the lowest-cost supplier of this kind of medicine. So Harry got creative. As soon as the vendor refused to negotiate with him, he set out to provide his own supply of pig thyroid and bypass his vendor entirely. It took two years, but he has now started up his own pig thyroid processor and thus substantially lowered his direct costs. By taking control of production of this main ingredient, the business anticipates not only returning to but *exceeding* its former profit levels.

You're not in business alone—you're going to need raw materials, and you're going to need labor. You need to know who's in your pipeline of direct costs and whom you're relying on. If prices change drastically, you might have to be really creative.

KEY TIPS

- **Group costs into just a few line items.** I have a client who was listing five different kinds of auto expenses on his P&L when he first came in. He was tracking gas versus routine maintenance versus repairs versus tires versus insurance. It was too much. One category for auto expenses would suffice. You can always drill down into detail later, but for the P&L, keep it to a few main categories.
- **Track costs against your revenue lines.** Remember that your whole goal here is to determine profitability, so track costs against your revenue lines.
- **Compare percentages to keep them in line.** If your goal is to sell at 50% gross profit, track that number monthly to be sure you meet your target. Also track your marketing cost-to-revenue percentage to ensure you're getting a good ROI.

CHAPTER 13

EMPLOYING FOLKS

WHAT ARE YOUR LABOR COSTS?

Labor is often the biggest expense of a business, so managing this component of costs is critical.

Here's an example of what the labor costs might look like on a P&L:

Excerpt Service Payroll

	Jan–Dec 2017	Jan–Dec 2016	Change
	Payroll		
401(k) Match & Profit Sharing	25,735	31,177	(5,443)
Professionals	500,000	269,707	230,293
Administration	198,149	259,442	(61,294)
Bonus	51,803	24,453	27,350
Contract Services	9,900	31,659	(21,759)
Employee Expense Reimbursements	1,804	2,217	(413)
Health & Dental Insurance	52,583	54,105	(1,522)
Incentive Rewards	3,210	15,126	(11,916)
Life Insurance	2,701	860	1,841
Officer's Salary	75,772	85,682	(9,910)
Consulting Expense	180,006	43,000	137,006
Total Officer's Salary	255,778	128,682	127,096
Payroll Taxes	66,993	66,038	955
Professional Development	16,132	13,477	2,655
Recruiting	5,238	13,046	(7,808)
Staff Meals	9,612	7,769	1,843
Team Building	5,167	4,055	1,112
Workers' Comp	972	265	707
Total Payroll	**1,205,775**	**922,078**	**283,697**

AN EXTRA HOLIDAY AND UNLIMITED TIME OFF— HIDDEN LABOR COSTS

At the same time that eeCPA was experiencing a change

in management, we were revising our employee manual. The previous year, we'd given employees the day after Christmas off, so the employee in charge of drafting the manual ended up adding that day into the manual as an extra guaranteed holiday off. The new manager in place didn't know any better, so he assumed the draft was correct and signed off on it.

Just one extra day off doesn't sound like a big deal, right? Well, once we added up all the paid time off and lost opportunity cost from not working, the cost of this mistake ended up being $5,000. An extra $5,000 can impact your business, especially if it's an unanticipated cost.

Then in 2017, we tried offering unlimited paid time off. With the kind of business we're in, we often need people at critical dates, such as during tax season or during crunch time before the sale of a client's business. So unlimited paid time off is a trade-off with employees. They can take off as much time as they want, *but* when I need them to stay late and work weekends to get through crunch time, they put in the overtime.

Much to my chagrin, this approach ended up not working for us, as the benefit did not drive the behavior I was looking for. My lowest performers were the ones to take advantage of the unlimited nature of the paid time off, but their work performance did not improve in kind.

Meanwhile, my highest performers—the ones I wanted to reward—continued to always put in the time and effort when needed, but they took about the same number of vacation days as they got in the normal accrual system.

When I went through and calculated the total cost of trying out this new method, I discovered that it was close to $50,000. That amount of money wasn't worth the negligible employee performance improvements, so with the start of the new year, we switched back to the old method.

Labor is much more than just wages, so you have to keep track of the impact of all the costs associated with employing people. Otherwise, they can add up quickly and surprise you.

LABOR COSTS

Labor costs of course include the money you pay your employees, but it also includes benefits, human resources costs, finance costs, and payroll taxes. Don't forget about recruiting costs either. If you are scaling your business, you are likely continually adding new positions, and all the costs associated with obtaining new talent are part of labor costs too.

Labor costs can vary week to week depending on when people take vacation time, when taxes are due, and so on.

So to determine your average weekly labor cost, add up all your labor costs for the entire year and divide by fifty-two.

BENEFITS

What kind of benefits do you offer your employees? Many benefits are required by law. For example, in Arizona, a new sick-time law has gone into effect that entitles even part-time employees to as many as forty hours of sick pay per year. So that's a whole week you have to pay your employees for not working.

The following are some of the most common types of benefits that you need to factor into labor costs:

- paid time off—holidays, sick time, and vacation time
- insurance—health insurance, dental insurance, vision insurance, disability insurance, and life insurance
- retirement benefits, including 401(k) matching
- professional development/continuing education with tuition reimbursement

HUMAN RESOURCES

When you employ people, you also have to employ people to manage them. All salaries for management and human resources therefore fall under labor costs. It's beneficial to separate these costs out from your other employee wages so that you can see the cost of managing your employees.

FINANCE

When you employ people, you also need a system to pay those people. All your associated finance costs, including payroll software and the salary of the finance person who is processing the payroll, fall under labor costs.

PAYROLL TAXES

Payroll taxes (Social Security, Medicare, and federal and state unemployment taxes) also add to labor costs.

COMMON MISCONCEPTIONS ABOUT LABOR
MYTH #1: YOU CAN GET SOMEONE FOR $10 AN HOUR

For a lot of jobs, $10 an hour isn't going to get you someone qualified. A lot of people think they can get a bookkeeper to run their office for $10 an hour, but at that rate, how effective is that person likely going to be? If you find out later that they don't have the skills required to do the job, you will have to fire them and hire someone new, and if they *are* good at their job, it is only a matter of time before they leave to work at someplace that will pay them according to their skills.

Employee turnover like this can be quite costly, as there are a lot of soft costs associated with employing people that you might not be considering. Every time you hire an employee, you have to go through an onboarding process, and every time you fire an employee, you have to go through an offboarding process. Both cost time and money.

Oftentimes, it takes at least ninety days to get new employees to the point where they can work independently. Until that time, the new employees won't be fully contributing to the efforts of the company, and veteran employees will have to take time away from their normal duties to train the new employees. Even once new employees can work independently, it can then take up to an additional full year or more for them to become totally familiar with the company, to the point where they begin thinking beyond their normal work duties and become a greater contribution to the organization as a whole.

If you are insisting on paying below market rate, you have to ask yourself, what kind of deal are you really getting? If you're focused only on getting a deal instead of on getting good employees, you're going to experience high turnover, and you won't get the best bang for your buck. A $10/hour employee tends to cost much more than that when you factor in the associated soft costs of training, supervisory time, onboarding time, and offboarding time.

MYTH #2: REMOTE WORKERS COST THE SAME AS IN-HOUSE WORKERS

If you're hiring remote workers (actual employees, not independent contractors) from another state, there will be additional costs you need to consider.

For one, having that out-of-state worker might establish nexus for your business in that state. You will then have to register to do business in that state, may have to pay state income taxes in that state, and will have to comply with that state's labor laws. Different states have different rules and requirements related to labor, different unemployment rates, different taxes, and different fees and licenses.

So if your business is located in Arizona and you're employing a person in Arizona, you just have to add together that person's salary, payroll taxes, benefits, and a share of the human resources and finance overhead to determine the cost of employing that person. But if that person is in another state, then you also have to take into account the cost of registering to do business in that state as well as the cost (in time and money) of becoming familiar with and complying with the laws of that state.

I don't mean to scare you away from out-of-state employees. I personally have out-of-state employees and contractors in Montana, Georgia, and Connecticut.

You just need to be aware of the full cost of employing those people.

THE IMPORTANCE OF GOOD EMPLOYEES

Employees can make or break a business, so you absolutely must make proper hiring decisions. According to a recent CareerBuilder survey, the average cost of one bad hire is nearly $15,000.[5] Hiring the right person in the beginning will save you time and money in the long run.

Just as important as hiring the right people is retaining them. Turnover is a huge cost to a company in both financial and company culture terms. The CareerBuilder survey mentioned above found that the average cost of losing a good hire is almost $30,000.[6] With low employee retention, you have to spend more time interviewing and training new hires. For me, with our ramp-up process, it usually takes a full year for me to realize the value of a new hire. A year is a long time to commit to an employee, so I focus a lot of attention on the hiring process to make sure I'm bringing in good people and getting an ROI on my hiring decisions.

---

[5] "Nearly Three in Four Employers Affected by a Bad Hire, according to a Recent CareerBuilder Survey," CareerBuilder, December 7, 2017, http://press.careerbuilder.com/2017-12-07-Nearly-Three-in-Four-Employers-Affected-by-a-Bad-Hire-According-to-a-Recent-CareerBuilder-Survey.

[6] Ibid.

A big part of ensuring I'm hiring the right people is doing background checks. As I discussed previously, you want to not only run criminal and credit report background checks (to help protect against potential embezzlement and fraud) but also check potential new hire's qualifications. According to HireRight's *2017 Employment Screening Benchmark Report*, a whopping 85% of employers caught applicants fibbing on their résumés or applications, up from just 66% five years ago.[7] Without background checks, you could hire someone who has a history of embezzlement or other criminal activity or someone who has misrepresented their qualifications and will make a lot of costly mistakes. Either of these situations will expose the company and potentially your clients to a huge risk.

Businesses lose money when employees are inefficient, so establish ways to track your employee efficiency. You can do customer satisfaction surveys, look at sales numbers, analyze work output, or a number of other things depending on your specific business.

Ideally, you will make the right hire in the beginning, but you're not going to be right 100% of the time. According to that recent CareerBuilder survey, two in three workers say they have accepted a job and later realized it was a bad fit. Half of these workers quit within six months,

---

7   *2017 Employment Screening Benchmark Report* (Irvine, CA: HireRight, 2017).

contributing to turnover costs. More than a third (37%) stick it out, but I imagine they are not the most productive employees, contributing to costs in other ways.[8]

When you discover an employee is inefficient or isn't the right fit, act quickly. Sometimes that means letting that employee go and getting someone new in the position, and sometimes it means providing more training to increase efficiency. Other times, it might mean cutting back that employee's hours because there's not enough work to justify another employee.

Part of tracking employee efficiency is matching employee costs against corresponding revenue. For example, if you had two salespeople last year bringing in $1 million worth of revenue and then you hire a third, potentially you should be able to do $1.5 million in revenue. Let's say the full labor costs of hiring that new person come to $250,000, but then yearly revenue rises to only $1.2 million after their hire. Obviously, you have a problem and should investigate. Maybe that person needs additional training or isn't the right fit, or maybe there's not enough work to justify a third full-time salesperson and you need to cut them back to part time.

Tracking efficiency can be especially difficult with remote workers. In a physical setting, you can often see if some-

---

[8] "Nearly Three in Four Employers," CareerBuilder.

one is clearly slacking off and not working, but you can't do that with remote workers. As a result, sometimes you're better off paying by the project than by the hour with remote workers.

Your business can't function without your employees. You want efficient, qualified people working for you, so work to make good hires.

BEST PRACTICES: HOW TO MANAGE LABOR COSTS
CALCULATE THE TRUE COSTS OF HIRING AND ONBOARDING AN EMPLOYEE

The next time you need to hire an employee, take the time to track the full costs of hiring and onboarding that person.

Begin tracking from when you first draft the job posting or ask someone for a recommendation. How much time and resources go into finding applicants, reviewing applications, conducting interviews, running background checks, and then finally making the hire? Be sure to factor in the administrative costs and time, such as doing all the onboarding paperwork, giving the employee a building keycard and ID badge, and so on.

Then track how long it takes the new hire to become

independent. How much training does the new employee go through, and how many people are involved in the training process? How long are the trainer employees removed from their workload to train the new employee?

With all this information, you can calculate and evaluate the true cost of bringing on a new hire. You might be surprised at how many resources you're investing into the hiring and onboarding process. You may find places where you can increase efficiency, or you may realize that you need to focus on higher employee retention to avoid incurring these onboarding costs.

CALCULATE ALL COSTS ASSOCIATED WITH EMPLOYEES

Labor costs are more than just payroll and payroll taxes. In fact, an employee's wages account for only about two-thirds of their total labor cost. There are a number of labor overhead costs you must consider:

- employee benefits, which were detailed earlier (pay special attention to health insurance and paid-time-off costs, as those both add up quickly)
- team-building events
- meals (e.g., ordering in lunch as a special treat)
- incentives, awards, and bonuses (e.g., handing out

gift cards to reward work performance or giving holiday bonuses)
- supplies and tools (e.g., workstations, desk, and software licenses)

To determine the average labor overhead cost for an employee, add all these costs up, and divide by the average number of employees you had during the year. (Alternatively, you could add all your labor costs up, subtract wages and payroll taxes, and then divide by the average number of employees to get the average labor overhead cost per employee.) Then, to calculate the full labor costs for a particular employee, you should add together that employee's wages, plus 10% for payroll taxes, plus the average labor overhead cost per employee.

TRACK PERFORMANCE

The first step to tracking performance is having checklists in place for your various processes. This way, everyone will be doing things the same way, so you can easily compare performance. Having checklists also makes it easier to train new employees, as checklists give new hires clear steps to follow.

Then verify that your employees are doing their jobs. If you use some kind of workflow software, you can review your employees' various tasks and checklists to ensure that they're being completed. At eeCPA, we use the app Process Street to do this. We also use Asana to track all our projects and tasks for fulfillment, along with Everhour to track time by team member by project/client. We then pull all the information into Slemma to create dashboards to alert management about overdue or overbudget tasks. In addition to reviewing your employees' day-to-day work through apps and software, ask for a monthly report from your team. You can also hire a consultant if you have the budget for it to evaluate the efficiency of your employees.

I made the mistake once of not verifying that one of my employees was doing his job. He always seemed to be hard at work, toiling away on his assigned tax returns, rarely leaving his computer. Five days before the tax deadline, I asked him for the tax returns that were ready to be filed. At the end of the workday, he came into my office, dumped thirty files on my desk (this was before we went paperless), and said, "Here you go. I haven't gotten to any of these. You gave me way too much to do."

At that point, a lot of expletives ran through my mind. I had no idea he was so behind. If one of my employees is struggling and overwhelmed, I work with them to find a solution, but this wasn't a case of a hardworking employee with too much to do. This was laziness—pure and simple. This CPA hadn't even tried to do his assigned work, and he'd said nothing to anyone about it. And now we had only four days before all these returns were due.

I went home that night and got essentially no sleep due to stress. The next morning, I came back in, let him go, and then buckled down to finish the files. I didn't leave the office for the next four days. I worked nonstop. I took naps on the office couch from one to three in the morning and then went back to work, because I had to finish these tax returns before the deadline.

At two o'clock one morning during that four-day stint, I started wondering, with some more expletives thrown in, what exactly this employee had been doing this whole time if he hadn't been doing his work. I went into his office and pored over his files, and then I checked his computer history. It turned out that he had been playing videos games and fantasy football most of the time.

I was furious, mostly at him but also at myself for not paying closer attention and realizing that he'd been screwing around for months. I hadn't put a good management team into place yet, and I had too much on my plate to do that job well enough myself. I definitely learned my lesson and immediately started taking steps to build my management team.

I've been employing people since I was eighteen, and you

would never imagine some of the things people will do. Fostering good employees and watching them grow and succeed can be very rewarding, but dealing with the bad ones can be downright traumatizing. My blood still boils when I think about that guy.

Even if you think you've made a great hire, you need to track employee performance and verify that people are doing their jobs. Take it from me: you can save yourself a lot of stress by properly managing your employees.

ANALYZE WHETHER TO HIRE OR OUTSOURCE

When you're deciding between hiring and outsourcing for a particular job, ask yourself these questions:

- Is there enough work to justify a part-time or full-time hire to take care of it?
- Can I afford to hire someone full time or part time to do this work?
- Can I find and retain the right people?
- Do I have the appropriate resources to train them and monitor their performance?
- Do I have the tools and materials for them to do their job?

If you answer yes to all these questions, then hiring is

likely a good option for you, but if you answer no to any of them, you should consider outsourcing.

Especially when you first start out, you may need some services but won't have enough work to justify a full-time employee. Outsourcing is less commitment than hiring an employee. When you outsource, you only pay for the time the outsourced people actually work; if you hire people in, you have to pay them for a guaranteed number of hours, even if they have nothing to do and sit idle for hours at a time.

It can be very convenient to use outsourcing as a turn-it-on, turn-it-off type of service. For example, the company that recently installed a new security system in my office outsources some of their labor needs. The owner used to have a number of employees, but during the recession, he had to let lots of them go. Now he keeps just one crew, and he contracts out with a labor pool company as he needs extra help. When he can build up enough work for a whole second crew full time, he'll hire in-house employees. Until then, he'll keep outsourcing.

Even as you scale, often you'll need several different types of service, all at a minimally part-time level. When you outsource, you can leverage your resources to get a number of different services for a bundled price. Maybe hiring one single person in-house would be cheaper, but by outsourcing, you can get a team of top-notch experts to complete five different services for you instead of relying on one person who is good at only one of those services and mediocre at the rest.

For example, you could hire an in-house IT specialist. However, if that employee is out and the computer system goes down, you will have to find an emergency solution, potentially putting your whole business at risk. With all the hackers and viruses out there today, as constantly highlighted in the news, the better solution might be hiring an IT company that provides 24-7 support for your business. While the IT specialist alone might be cheaper, the outsourced rate to maintain your systems and continually monitor them provides much more bang for your buck than relying on one person who may or may not be available when the virus strikes.

Eventually, you will reach the point where it makes sense (and you can afford) to build your own in-house team of all the professionals you need, but until then, outsourcing will usually give you more bang for your buck—better quality of service for a lower price. For example, hiring a trained, experienced CPA is going to cost at least $100,000 annually for salary alone, but if you outsource that work, you can likely get the job done for $75,000, because you can take advantage of hiring a whole team with multiple-tiered billing rates and levels of expertise.

Outsourcing can also be beneficial if you don't know enough about a particular service to know whether the person you're hiring is truly qualified. If you don't understand finance, for example, and place your trust in a $10/hour bookkeeper or even a $100,000/year CFO who assures you they're qualified, it could come back to bite you later. I have horror story upon horror story of bad CFOs who embezzled millions or who drove companies into the ground through incompetence. When you outsource, the company you outsource to is responsible for finding qualified people, and they're typically pretty darn good at it, because they do it day in and day out.

Outsourcing is also smart if you don't have the time or resources to properly manage the new employee. Because I didn't have the time to properly manage that lazy CPA who made four days of my life a living hell, I would have been better off outsourcing that work until I could afford to put a management team in place. That way, whatever company I outsourced to would have been responsible for managing him and making sure he did his job.

Having an outsourced company manage the needed labor also means you don't have to worry about employee absences. If a key employee calls out sick during crunch time, it can set you back quite a bit. If you're outsourcing, though, the outsourced company will take care of all hiccups like this, as they're guaranteeing to have someone qualified available to do the work at the agreed-upon times.

Finally, outsourcing is also valuable if you don't have the tools or resources an employee needs to do their job. Are you willing to pay for a bunch of new equipment or licensing fees? For example, licensed CPAs are required to complete forty hours of continuing professional education per year. If you require that certification for your employee, it's expected that you will pay for the continuing professional education costs. Are you willing to do that?

If you do decide to outsource, make sure to outsource to someone who gives you a service guarantee. (Good luck trying to get a service guarantee with an employee!) If one of your employees makes a costly mistake, you can fire them, but you can't recoup any losses. If you outsource to someplace with a service guarantee and something goes wrong, you have recourse.

When you need a new service of some kind at your company, it's worth analyzing the pros and cons of either outsourcing or hiring someone in. More often than you think, outsourcing is the best solution.

KEY TIPS

- **Make good hires.** A lot of time and money goes into hiring and onboarding employees, so you want to pick the right people. Draft an accurate, engaging job description to attract the right candidates and do thorough background checks.
- **Track efficiency.** In a restaurant, you can send a waiter home when the tables are empty, but in an office without parameters, it's difficult to see where inefficiencies are unless you have systems in place. Set clear expectations for each position within your company and track and evaluate performance according to those expectations.
- **Compare the costs and benefits of either outsourcing or hiring.** You want to get the most mileage out of your money, and with all the labor overhead costs (which typically account for about one-third of total labor costs), sometimes that means outsourcing instead of hiring in-house employees.

CHAPTER 14

RUNNING THE BUSINESS

WHAT ARE YOUR GENERAL AND ADMINISTRATIVE COSTS AND OCCUPANCY COSTS?

The last major categories of your P&L are your general and administrative costs and your occupancy costs. Here's what those sections might look like on the P&L:

G&A Expenses

	Jan–Dec 2017	Jan–Dec 2016	Change
General & Admin Costs			
Auto Expense	13,127	8,452	4,675
Bad Debt Expense	-	46,783	(46,783)
Bank Charges & Merchant Fees	18,064	18,986	(922)
Charity	190		190
Dues & Subscriptions	7,256	3,735	3,522
Insurance	15,630	15,137	493
Interest Expense	2,253	912	1,342
Licenses & Permits	471	585	(114)
Miscellaneous	125	627	(502)
Office Expenses	17,263	26,994	(9,731)
Parking	218		218
Postage and Delivery	4,290	4,747	(457)
Professional Fees	14,649	3,512	11,137
Resource Materials	1,603	812	790
Telephone & Internet	20,829	22,753	(1,924)
Total General & Admin Costs	**115,969**	**154,036**	**(38,067)**

THE LITTLE COSTS YOU DON'T NOTICE UNTIL YOU HAVE NO INCOME COMING IN—MY EXPERIENCE BEING ROBBED

One day in 2006, I woke up at five in the morning to a call from the Scottsdale police. My office had been robbed. I drove over to the office and walked inside to see the damage. Nearly everything had been stolen, including all my computers and backup devices. Some furniture was all that was left, and it had been completely trashed, broken apart to get inside locked compartments. *Wow!* (Well, it wasn't really *wow*, it was more like *$#@*!*) I thought, *I am screwed*. Then I went home and drank a bottle of vodka. I was completely devastated. At this same time, I was going through a divorce and a custody battle, so this was just the icing on a moldy cake.

Luckily, I had an online backup for all my files, which was unusual for 2006. None of the major cloud services we're used to today—for example, Apple Cloud, Dropbox, and Google Drive—existed at that point. Thank God I had subscribed to this online backup service. If I hadn't, I would have lost everything.

But while I luckily still had access to all these file, so did someone else, which was a major issue. There was a ton of sensitive financial information on those computers and in my office that some unknown person now possessed. I also had signatory authority on some of my clients' accounts, so I had checkbooks for those accounts in a locked drawer in my desk. The thief had broken apart the desk and stolen those checkbooks along with everything else, which meant he now had access to some of my clients' checking accounts. You understand that bottle of vodka now, right?

Because of the loss of sensitive data and checkbooks, I

had to immediately notify all my clients, some of whom had to freeze accounts and then open up new accounts, and I also had to get the FBI involved.

Conservatively, I lost $50,000 in stolen and damaged materials, and that doesn't include all the time and money I lost trying to recover from the theft. The robbery shut me down for weeks. I had the online backup, but I couldn't use it until I bought new computers, and I couldn't buy new equipment until I upgraded our security system.

Every single day I would call the police to see if they had made any progress on the investigation. And then somehow everything managed to get even worse.

A week or two after the robbery, I got a call from someone who said they were from Wells Fargo. They told me someone was trying to cash a check on one of the accounts with stolen checkbooks. "Do you want to come down?" they asked.

"Absolutely," I said, and I ran out to my car.

Sitting there inside my car, on the dashboard, was a packet. The thief had put it there, using the extra key to my car that he'd stolen from my office. A note on the packet said, "Go straight to the bank. Withdraw $10,000, meet us at the Village Inn, and then wait for instructions. We're watching you. You can get your computers back." I realized then that the call from Wells Fargo was fake. I was terrified. Now the thief had invaded my personal life in addition to my professional life.

I drove to the bank and withdrew the money. Then I drove to the police station. The police were going to send a decoy to the meeting point, but they didn't have anyone that looked like me. So I had to drive my car to meet the thief while a policeman was lying down in the back. It felt like a Lifetime movie. When we got to the drop-off point, no one was there. The thief must've gotten spooked because it took me so long at the police station to get everything together. So that was a needlessly terrifying dead end.

A week or two later, though, while conducting a drug raid at a neighboring home, the police found a lot of the computers and equipment, and eventually, they did catch the guy. The thief was trying to pawn the computers and equipment at different pawn shops, and many of the pawn shops were calling in to the police about him because the equipment was flagged as stolen merchandise in the pawn shop database system. He was also writing checks out of the stolen checkbooks to himself, which wasn't very smart, but he was on crystal meth and not making the best decisions.

The time from 2006 to 2007 was horrible. Several months after he was caught, I testified at his court hearing. I was pregnant and still working through my divorce at this time, and I was in tears as I testified. I wasn't the only one. I don't think there was a dry eye in the courtroom. "All I do is work and take care of my kids," I said, "and he destroyed my life and my business that I worked so hard for."

The man got nine years for the robbery, and I got a $36,000 judgment against him, on which I've collected about $200. He's out of prison now. He probably left the state, and he's probably working but getting paid under the table, so his wages can't be garnished to pay my judgment.

Thankfully, I had a fantastic reputation, so I didn't lose any clients from the whole fiasco, but everyone was understandably freaked out because all their personal information had been stolen. I turned in an insurance claim for the $50,000 loss, but the insurance covered only $14,000. Insurance companies fight tooth and nail over every penny and depreciate everything heavily, so they never pay you back the whole amount you've lost. I had to argue and argue, and $14,000 was all I could get.

I had a $36,000 loss I couldn't do anything about, so I had to immediately get back to work. Luckily, I had strong relationships with my vendors, and they helped finance me through this time, letting me stretch out payment terms. I also had a cash reserve, which was a godsend. Even with my cash reserve, it took me years to get back on my feet after the robbery, but without this reserve, I never would have been able to bounce back. This is a prime example of how an adequate cash reserve can make or break your business!

I wasn't quite so lucky when it came to my general and administrative costs and my occupancy costs. In order to keep doing business, I had to keep paying my rent, utilities, insurance premiums, subscription fees, and the like. While I was able to negotiate favorable payment terms on many other costs, a lot of my occupancy costs and general and administrative costs were nonnegotiable. For instance, either I paid my utilities bill when it was due, or I wouldn't have air-conditioning.

Now that I was paying attention to every single cost, though, I discovered some waste in this area and was able to cut back on unnecessary spending. It's easy to brush occupancy costs and general and administrative costs aside when business is booming, but once you're put in the place of having to rebuild from the ground up, you truly understand how these costs can add up.

GENERAL AND ADMINISTRATIVE COSTS AND OCCUPANCY COSTS

General and administrative costs include auto expenses, dues and subscriptions, licenses and permits, insurance, professional fees, and office expenses.

Occupancy costs include rent or lease payments, utilities, and insurance.

All these costs are things that aren't directly linked to the sale, but they are required to run your business. If you don't pay your rent, you have nowhere to do business. If you don't pay your utilities, they'll be turned off, and most businesses don't operate well in the dark. If you don't pay for your software and licensing fees, you'll have no way to complete your work.

It is important that you look at what all these costs are as a percentage of revenue, and then you must factor in these costs when determining your break-even point and subsequent pricing structure. These costs are nearly always fixed, and they might be small in comparison to your direct costs and payroll, but they add up.

The lower you can keep your general and administrative costs and occupancy costs, the less revenue you have to make to be profitable.

COMMON MISCONCEPTIONS ABOUT GENERAL AND ADMINISTRATIVE COSTS AND OCCUPANCY COSTS

MYTH #1: IT'S JUST A LITTLE EXPENSE

As you get busy, it's easy to lose sight of all these miscellaneous fixed costs. You think, *Oh, it's only twenty-five bucks a month. It's not worth my time right now.* But with twenty-five bucks here, fifty there, two hundred there, and on and on, these costs add up. These costs don't directly drive revenue, so if you're spending unnecessary money in this category, you're essentially throwing that money away.

Think about coffee. Seems like a negligible expense, right? Well, in my office, someone wanted caramel coffee, someone else wanted hazelnut, and yet another person wanted Tazo tea. Pretty soon, we had fifteen different boxes of Keurig K-Cups for the fifteen different people in the office. Because we needed so many different kinds of coffee and tea, we were buying smaller packages, which meant a higher per-K-Cup price—almost twice as much as if we were buying in bulk. Over the course of a month, this added up to an extra $200 per month in overspending just on coffee.

Maybe a couple of hundred bucks doesn't seem that important compared to the hundreds of thousands of dollars spent on payroll, but you wouldn't turn down an extra $2,400 in your pocket every year, would you?

MYTH #2: INSURANCE IS FULL PROTECTION

You should absolutely have insurance, but as I discovered firsthand, it will not cover everything. In my case, it paid less than a third of what I lost. It wasn't as much as I wanted, but it was still a help.

The issue is that as soon as you buy something, it begins depreciating. That computer you bought five years ago? It's worth almost nothing now because of depreciation. If you need to replace it, though, you will have to shell out hundreds of dollars for a new one.

So invest in insurance, but don't expect it to cover everything. Have cash reserves and a line of credit available for emergencies and worst-case scenarios, such as robberies.

Also, be sure to carefully review all insurance contracts. One of my clients recently suffered a fire, and when he tried to make an insurance claim, he discovered that he had only liability and workers' compensation coverage. Everything he'd lost in the fire wasn't covered. You absolutely must understand what exactly your insurance covers. You may wish to consult a professional to ensure you have adequate coverage.

OCCUPANCY CONSIDERATIONS
LEASING VERSUS BUYING

One of the most important decisions you will make in relation to occupancy costs is whether to lease or buy. There are pros and cons to each.

Leasing

Pros

- low commitment, high flexibility
- no large down payment up front
- no unexpected repair or maintenance costs
- property manager to handle logistics

Cons

- hassle of lease renewals, including potential price increases
- no equity
- cost of leasehold improvements, which you will no longer benefit from once your lease ends
- less control over space

Buying

Pros

- equity, including potential appreciation and increase in value

- stability, including long-term fixed overhead costs
- complete control over space
- no leasehold improvement costs you must later walk away from

Cons

- high commitment, low flexibility
- large down payment needed
- repair and maintenance costs
- no property manager to handle any issues that crop up (that means *you* get to do it!)

When deciding whether to lease or buy, start by determining what your resources are. If you don't have the capital for a down payment, then you're not going to be buying. You also need to think about the cost of any improvements you want to make to the building. If you're leasing, you can get your landlord to finance tenant improvements for you. If you buy, you will be responsible for paying for such improvements yourself. Do you have a budget for that?

Then look at your plan for the business. Are you planning on staying in this location? Are you planning on expanding? If you expect big changes or are unsure what the future holds for your business, leasing can be a better option. This way, if you need to move locations or either downsize or upgrade your space, you don't have to worry about selling your current building; you just find a new location once your lease is up.

When making the lease-versus-buy decision, you should do a monthly and yearly cost comparison and also look at the future payoff potential.

Buying—Pros and Cons

Buying is a long-term investment, and depending on location and a host of other factors, it can be more affordable in the long term, especially in a low-interest-rate environment. When you buy, you can write off and depreciate the building, and you will be building equity. With the potential for appreciation, you could even make quite a bit of money off the purchase.

Earlier, I talked about a real estate sale I helped facilitate for a client. In that case, the client had originally bought the property during the downturn in 2009 for $14.2 million and then sold it in 2016 for about $30 million. In that time, they made a couple of million dollars of improvements, but the vast majority of that almost $16 million increase in value was due just to appreciation. Pretty good ROI!

But remember that this can work in the opposite direction too. You could purchase a building for $1 million today, but if the real estate market declines due to rising interest rates or an economic recession, the building could lose value and may drop to just $800,000 by next year.

Buying is a greater commitment. It is a mostly permanent decision, so there is often more risk, which means potentially greater rewards but also potentially greater losses. Your business doubles in size and you need more space? Too bad. The neighborhood you're in starts declining? Too bad. Have to spend tens of thousands of dollars replacing the roof? Too bad.

When you buy, you're entering into the whole different business of real estate, which you may or may not be equipped to do. You may have to lease some of the space to tenants. Are you prepared to do that? Are you prepared to manage a building when things break down and things go wrong?

While you're responsible for a lot more when you own, such as all the repair and maintenance costs, you also get a lot more control and stability as a result. You can make whatever alterations you want to the space, and you can control your overhead costs. You don't have to worry about your landlord increasing your rent, because you are your own landlord.

Even if you're a smaller business, buying can make sense

for you. I have a law firm client that does only a few hundred thousand dollars a year, and they bought a building a couple of years ago. It has worked out very well for them. They can control their rent costs, and they've gotten to design their space exactly as they want it.

If you decide buying is the best option for you, I recommend setting up another LLC to own the building and having your business pay rent to that LLC. This structure will protect you from liability and help keep the business and building separate, so if you ever want to sell the business or the building individually, you can easily facilitate the sales transaction.

Leasing—Pros and Cons

With leasing, all the pros and cons of buying are reversed. You're not responsible for repair and maintenance costs, you don't have to tie up your cash with a down payment, and you're committed to a space only for the length of your lease. In exchange, you have less control over what you can do to the space, you have to deal with lease renewals, and you don't build any equity. Plus, you must walk away from any investment in tenant improvements once the lease expires.

Back in 2012, I was looking at buying an office condo, but I ended up deciding not to because I didn't want to deal with the association fees and if I needed to rent that space out for any reason, it would be more difficult to get tenants for a condo office space than a traditional office space. Instead, I signed a five-and-a-half-year lease. I invested probably $70,000 in tenant improvements over the course of that lease. We utilized those improvements while we were there, but I didn't get to take those improvements with me when I left the lease. So that $70,000 became lost money—it contributed to the landlord's equity, not my own equity.

I've now purchased my own building, and looking back, I wish I would've bought a building in 2012 so that I could have been building equity. But back in 2012, I wasn't willing to take on the risk, so I stand by the decision.

If you choose to lease, you need to put thought into your lease length. I had a client back in 2009 who had signed a long-term lease for a decent amount of space, as the business was growing rapidly. Then the company changed direction and cut back their team. Suddenly, they were stuck paying $1 million a year renting space they weren't fully utilizing. Having empty space at $1 million a year adds up quickly, so if you do have a longer-term lease and find yourself stuck with extra space, be proactive in subleasing that unutilized space to conserve the company's resources.

Obviously, in this scenario, a shorter-term lease would

have been better. Shorter-term leases give you more flexibility and freedom to either grow and expand or cut back as needed. However, long-term leases can be more cost effective, and a lot of commercial landlords will offer only long-term leases, especially if you want your landlord to finance any leasehold improvements for you.

Shorter-term leases also mean that lease renewals will come up more frequently, meaning more potential for price increases and more hassle related to negotiations. I've seen a lot of companies go out of business because of leases expiring at an inopportune time for their business. If you're stuck renegotiating at a critical time for your business, you're largely at the whim of your landlord. You're a sitting duck in the tenant seat and don't have a lot of leveraging power.

Ultimately, deciding whether to lease or buy is a pretty complex decision. It depends on so many different facts and circumstances. It's definitely worth spending a few thousand dollars on a high-level analysis to help you make the decision.

You should also establish an exit strategy or backup plan in case things don't work out. For example, maybe you commit to a ten-year lease for ten thousand square feet because you think your business will grow into it. You're betting on that growth happening, but if it doesn't, what's your plan? Will you have enough resources to continue to honor that lease? Do you have a plan to either sublet or get out of your lease in a worst-case scenario?

Committing to a location is like walking a tightrope. You don't want to be stuck with too little or too much space, so you have to make this decision carefully.

TAX-FREE LOCATIONS

A lot of business owners want to organize their business in a tax-free state, such as Nevada. After all, who doesn't want to lower their tax bill? However, it's not as easy as simply organizing in a tax-free state; you have to conduct all your business there too.

Even if you are headquartered in Nevada, for instance, if you establish nexus—or sufficient physical presence—in another state, you will have to pay taxes in that state. Having employees, owned or leased space, or equipment in another state will establish nexus, and then you will have to pay tax on any income earned in that state.

So before you buy or lease property in another state, understand that you may be triggering potential tax consequences. Also, keep in mind the different rules and licensing implications of doing business in another state.

For example, a lot of Arizona businesses want to expand to California while keeping their headquarters in Arizona, where the income tax rate is less than 5% (versus up to 13% in California). But as mentioned previously, California has different tax laws. In Arizona, once an LLC organizes, there are no continued filing fees or obligations to maintain their corporate structure, but if you're doing business in California, even if your headquarters is elsewhere, you have to pay a minimum franchise tax of $800 a year as an LLC, with additional taxes on top of that.

Because every state has different laws, it's a smart idea to sit down with a consultant and explore all the potential tax implications before scaling your business into another state.

BEST PRACTICES: HOW TO MANAGE GENERAL AND ADMINISTRATIVE EXPENSES

TRACK EXPENSES AND ESTABLISH PROCUREMENT PRACTICES

As with anything else, if you're not tracking your general and administrative expenses, there is no way for you to know what you're spending. Toilet paper, ink cartridges, highlighters, coffee—individually, these things seems like nickel-and-dime stuff, but they add up.

To make these expenses easier to track, put good procurement strategies in place. Designate who can make these purchases and limit the frequency of orders. If you have fifteen different employees making purchases on Amazon throughout the week, those expenses will be much harder to track than if you have a single person placing one large order each month.

You should also limit how much employees can spend in this area, with an approvals process for anything over that amount. You might think the budget for these items should be obvious, but you'd be surprised. I had a client who bought an original piece of art while traveling in Europe. She asked her assistant to get it framed, telling him, "The artwork was worth only $250, so let's not go crazy on the framing." He got it framed, and guess how much he spent: more than $400. The frame cost more than the artwork! My client was upset, but she took responsibility for the mistake and realized that she would need to set a specific budget with him in future situations like this.

To help avoid overspending, give your purchasing or procurement department a specific monthly budget to work with and have them submit reports about how they're doing against their budget.

Encouraging open lines of communication can also help limit overspending. All the time, issues arise just because people aren't communicating. Maybe Becca notices you're almost out of ink cartridges, so she orders new ones, but then later that week, Tim also orders new ones. Now you have twice as many as you need.

Just the other day in my office, I had to deal with a problem like this. When we moved offices, we had our plant guys take all our plants and put them in storage so they wouldn't be damaged by all the construction going on. Then, the other day, when the plant people called about bringing the plants back out, the person on my team who took the call said, "Oh yeah, deliver them," but didn't tell anyone else what was happening. So when the plant people arrived, the manager on site had no idea what was going on and told them to just put the plants in the corner. When I came in later that day, I had a bunch of giant potted plants—some exceeding one hundred pounds each—all crowded together in the corner. I sure as hell wasn't going to be hauling those around the office myself to place them, so I had to call the plant people back out. The extra trip cost us another $45, which, yes, isn't that much, but it was a completely unnecessary expense that could've been avoided had proper planning gone into place.

You won't be able to avoid every single unnecessary cost, but putting proactive strategies in place and tracking expenses will go a long way to limiting overspending.

PERFORM OCCASIONAL AUDITS AND LOOK FOR WAYS TO SAVE

To keep general and administrative costs and occupancy costs in check, periodically audit what you're spending in this category and look for ways to save. I recommend doing an overhaul review of these expenses at least once a year, and monthly is even better.

Evaluate your office expenses budget. Do you need to have six different kinds of sticky notes?

Pay special attention to all recurring charges. If you're no longer using a subscription, get rid of it! Watch out for auto-renewals and price increases, and also keep an eye on your software licenses. Some software might cost $75 per user per month. As part of your employee offboarding process, you need to go into your software licensing and either mark that subscription as ended or replace the user. Otherwise, you could be paying fees for months for people who no longer work for you.

Finally, once a year, evaluate your key vendor contracts. Renegotiate prices and get outside quotes for your more costly services (e.g., insurance, internet, etc.) to make sure you're getting the best value.

KEY TIPS

- **Pay attention to the small costs.** Every little bit you save in this area adds to your bottom line.
- **Do an analysis of the pros and cons of leasing versus buying before committing to a space.** Leasing and buying each come with their own benefits and risks, so you must assess your individual situation to determine the best solution for your needs.

CONCLUSION

NIGHTMARE TO DREAM—THE DIFFERENCE A GOOD ACCOUNTING SYSTEM MAKES

In 2010, I took on a niche software company as a new eeCPA client. The company, which had been started in 1989, sold specialized accounts receivable software to law firms. They had a good product, but they had no accounting system in place, no general ledger, nothing. When they called me, their bookkeeper had just quit, dropping off all their customer contracts, employee agreements, and various bills in a broken laundry basket.

The company was like a house of cards, with everything on the verge of collapsing. They were several years behind on their tax filing, had just come out of a huge lawsuit that required a change to their entire business model (they used to sell their software to another company, which then sold it to clients, but they now had to bring direct customer sales in-house), and were in the midst of launching a brand-new software product.

With everything going on, they were hemorrhaging money. They owed $600,000 in debts, and on average, the owners had to put in an additional $100,000 to $200,000 of seed money each year just to keep the business afloat.

We took them on as a client, and we immediately set them up with an accounting system. We reviewed every single contract they had—about five hundred—and started billing their customers and negotiating and collecting on their receivables. To streamline their business operations, they'd consolidated all their financial needs to our office as the outsourced provider, so we were also in charge of the payroll and HR functions. In this role, we put purchasing controls and salary schedules in place. Then we came up with a plan to repay their debt.

With the house of cards stabilized for the moment, we directed our efforts into building more revenue and generating more profit. First, we worked on supporting them to accelerate their new project launch so they could start capitalizing on that revenue. Then we made some small tweaks to their current business model that resulted in a big increase to the bottom line.

First, we changed their pricing structure. Their software required on-site training, and they had been offering this training to clients at $1,000 a day plus all the expenses (flights, meals, hotels, and so on). However, there was no system in place to record and keep track of these expenses, so many items were falling through the cracks and being charged to the business instead of the clients.

To remedy this issue, we created an expense reimbursement system for them. We opened a corporate credit account, gave each trainer a credit card, and then set up processes for the trainers on how to code and submit receipts for reimbursement. With a system in place, we soon realized that administratively managing this pricing approach was costing a lot of time and money. The customers tended to dispute the expense charges, demanding receipts and questioning why trainers had spent so much money on flights and meals instead of going for the bargain. These disputes caused a delay of game, and it often took ninety days or more to collect these expense reimbursements from the customers.

We proposed that instead of tracking and nitpicking all the individual expenses, the company sell the training service as an all-inclusive package. After reviewing and analyzing all the travel expenses, we determined that $1,500 a day would be an appropriate all-inclusive price ($500 more per day). The training took a week, so the whole training package would now cost $2,500 more than previously, but we were able to sell clients on the package idea by emphasizing the all-inclusive nature of the price. With the switch to an up-front flat fee for training, there were no more disputes over expenses, and there were no more delays in payment.

Next, we added price increases to the renewals process with customers. The company had annual maintenance agreements with their customers, but they never raised prices with these renewals. As a result, some customers had been paying the same price for ten to fifteen years. Meanwhile, the consumer price index had gone up, wages had gone up, and the business's direct costs had gone up. To cover these increased expenses, we proposed they increase their rates 5% per year with their renewal agreements. This 5% increase might mean an extra $50 on a $1,000 invoice. Naturally, some customers did give pushback, so sometimes we had to negotiate the increase down to 3% or even keep the rate the same in order to keep the customer. But in general, the price increases brought in money the business wouldn't otherwise have. (Approximately 90% of the customers paid the increase without inquiry.)

These two changes—the switch to a flat fee for training and the pricing increases—resulted in a 20% increase to the bottom line.

We also improved cash flow by adding a policy that customers had to pay deposits on the software. So if they committed to buying $100,000 of software, they had to pay $50,000 down and $50,000 when the training was completed. With this approach, the business received a steady cash flow instead of having to wait for months to collect on sales. We also added merchant services so they could get paid more quickly.

Then we cut a ton of costs, as the business was paying for a bunch of things they didn't need. For example, we got rid of unneeded leased space and changed their phone system to get a cheaper rate.

It took a couple of years, but with all these changes, by the end of 2012, they had paid off all $600,000 of debt. The business owners were also able to take dividends from the company for the first time in years. They began pulling $500,000 in dividends a year from the company on $3 million of revenue. We turned the company around from a loss of roughly 50% to a gain of 25%.

This huge shift almost seems impossible, but it's not. Sometimes you just need an extra set of eyes and someone managing your accounting system for you, and then you can realize these kinds of exponential returns pretty quickly.

At first, this client was put off by our fees. We were initially charging $15,000 a month and then dropped the fee down to $10,000 a month once we'd cleaned things up a bit. In comparison, they'd been paying their bookkeeper only around $1,000 a month. I understand why our fees seemed like a lot to them, but you have to look at the results. All the money they gave their bookkeeper essentially went down the drain, whereas the money they gave us resulted in a huge ROI to the company: we were able to generate profits in excess of four times the cost of our services. Wouldn't you invest $1,000 to get $5,000 back two years from now?

Also, before we came in, when they were selling their software to someone who then resold it, the other company took a 15% commission on all sales. So out of $3 million in revenue, they were receiving only $2.55 million, with $450,000 going to this middleman each year.

We were able to drive similar revenues for the company without charging a 15% commission on sales. Our services ended up giving them more profit than their previous business model had, at less than half the cost—$180,000 (for the first two years, after which it dropped down to $120,000 a year) versus $450,000.

Really, this company was getting a deal. In hindsight, I wish I would have priced this project as a success fee, where we would get 50% of whatever money we earned the company. If we'd done that, we would have made $250,000 (half of the new $500,000 of yearly profit) instead of $180,000.

In the end, the client was incredibly glad they had invested in our services. We were quite literally able to turn the entire company around, taking it from a loss to a profit and putting it in a position to succeed for years to come.

WHAT I WANT YOU TO REMEMBER
YOU MUST TRACK YOUR BUSINESS'S FINANCES

Imagine trying to shoot an arrow blindfolded. It will be pretty damn near impossible to hit the target, let alone the bull's-eye. If you don't know what is going on with your business, there is no way you can expect to spot costly mistakes or make the decisions that will lead to profit.

For instance, there are so many cool tax-planning strategies you can do with your company, but first you need to have current, accurate financial information. If you don't know how much cash you have, don't know what your current and long-term assets and liabilities are, don't know what your income and expenses are, or don't know what your break-even point is, then you can't even get to the stage of strategic decision-making.

You need a financial snapshot of your business—a picture

of where you stand today—to start the process of testing and tracking profit-making strategies to find what will work for you and bring you the greatest ROI. For example, donating land as a charitable expense or investing in a retirement plan could be useful tax-saving strategies for you, but you need to know when and how to apply them to maximize their effects. Your accounting system is what will give you the info you need to make smart decisions.

HAVE A FUTURE-LOOKING PLAN

Once you know where your business stands currently, make a plan for the future. Flying by the seat of your pants is never a good idea when running a business. If you're focused only on the next day, week, or month, your business won't be able to survive long term. As soon as you hit a single speed bump, everything will derail. You must plan for the future so that you can maximize profit, scale, and weather any storm that comes your way.

BECOME STRONG IN FORECASTING

To have the most effective future-looking plan, you need to be strong in forecasting.

Establish a baseline for your expected expenses, sales, and cash flow. Then draft both a conservative and an aggressive forecast. Your conservative forecast should be based on historical performance, while your aggressive forecast should be the ideal numbers you wish to achieve with your plans for the year.

Having these forecasts will allow you to measure your company's financial results against the plan and see where you may need to make changes to maintain consistency with your vision.

SYSTEMATIZE THINGS

Your accounting system is only as good as the information in it, so you must keep everything up to date and current. Do everything on a set schedule—billing your clients, recording bills, making purchases, everything.

So many issues come back to accounting and costs. If you systematize everything, putting set processes and procedures in place, you can ensure that things don't fall through the cracks and keep surprises to a minimum.

ADAPT WHEN NEEDED

Your business is a constantly moving, living, breathing entity. You absolutely need to have a plan and set procedures, but you also need to consistently compare the plan against the reality and adjust when needed. Treat your plan like a moving target. You want to stay true to your end game and vision, but sometimes you will need to modify your short-term strategies to realize your long-term vision.

INVEST IN YOUR ACCOUNTING SYSTEM

So many problems are manageable—from taxes, to embezzlement, to low profit, to debt—if you simply have a system in place.

If you don't have a financial system in place, your business will never perform as well as it could, and you won't be able to scale as effectively. Businesses with a plan and a system advance faster and do better, every single time. The single greatest thing you can do for your business is invest in your accounting system, so what are you waiting for? Get to work and start protecting your profit.

ACKNOWLEDGMENTS

A huge thank-you to Julie Arends, Barbara Boyd, and Kelsey Adams from Scribe Media for helping me refine my focus and develop my ideas and for asking the right questions to keep me on track (as best you could) toward the finish line.

Many thanks to my team at eeCPA. They have been awesome in supporting my vision to turn this book into a reality.

Thank you to all my clients who have continued to believe in me. By sharing your experiences and allowing me to partner with you to solve problems, I have learned so much. Your struggles and triumphs hit very close to home, and I could never have assembled the knowledge and experience that I have gained without you!

Finally, thank you to my extended family: Mom, Dad, Carolyn, Michael, Christopher, and Meredith. You have believed in me even when I did not believe in myself.

ABOUT THE AUTHOR

Elizabeth received her bachelor of science degree in accounting from St. John Fisher College in Rochester, New York, in 1993. She passed the CPA exam in November 1994 and became licensed to practice as a certified public accountant in Arizona in February 2003.

Elizabeth has been involved with small business from the age of eight. At eight years old, she responded to the back of a comic book ad for selling greeting cards door to door. She sold many boxes of holiday cards year after year, developing a list of loyal, repeat customers.

At age ten, she convinced her neighbor to allow her

to take on his paper route a year and a half before he planned on quitting. When she took over the route, she issued surveys to all her customers, asking them where exactly they would like the delivery made: front door, side door, mailbox? She followed up and never missed a delivery. She made sure that the papers never landed in a snowbank or puddle. Thus, she made substantial gratuities at holiday time.

Then, by age thirteen, she began work at her father's restaurant, a Prime Rib House in upstate New York. She worked at every job from dishwasher to brunch chef to hostess, server, and bartender. She loved serving the customers and made enough money to pay her own way through college!

When she got to college, Elizabeth began her studies in English and philosophy (after all, the 1980s was the liberal arts craze). After the first year, she determined that she needed to focus on a specific career that would translate into a real job, so she transitioned to the accounting major, keeping her minor in writing.

While finishing up her degree in the evenings, she served as a founder and controller for a regional service and wholesale distribution company. She started this business from nothing and grew it to almost $1 million in annual revenues. Ten years later (1999), she was able to sell it to a larger regional competitor for $1 million.

Today, Elizabeth Hale, CPA, has more than thirty years of experience working with small to medium businesses. Having owned or operated several small businesses, Elizabeth can readily communicate with her clients from a position of understanding how challenging it is to manage the vision, the employees, and the cash flow. Elizabeth has a passion for serving clients and being responsive to their needs. Consultancy provides her the opportunity to share and deepen her own expertise. Elizabeth founded eeCPA in 2004. Today, eeCPA employs fifteen dedicated team members to serve more than four hundred clients. Team eeCPA loves to simplify the complex and find creative solutions for the problems their clients face.

Elizabeth currently resides in Scottsdale with her children, Alexandria, Ryan, and Aspen, and soul mate, Robert. She enjoys swimming, hiking, reading, travel, and yoga.

PROFESSIONAL AFFILIATIONS

- Member of the American Institute of Certified Public Accountants
- Member of the Arizona Society of CPAs

BOARD POSITIONS

- Finance Director, Arizona Entrepreneurs' Organization (current)
- Treasurer and Fund-Raising Chair, Montessori School of Rochester (former)

APPENDIX

For additional resources, visit http://www.eecpa.com/protectyourprofit.

APPENDIX A:
Excellent Service Company Balance Sheet

	As of 12/31/17	As of 12/31/16	Change
ASSETS			
Current Assets			
Chase Checking 3906	13,295	44,661	(31,366)
Chase Money Market 4244	6,011	55,041	(49,030)
Petty Cash	40	495	(455)
Gift Cards	1,140	1,440	(300)
Total Cash	20,486	101,637	(81,151)
Accounts Receivable	146,343	68,462	77,881
Total Accounts Receivable	146,343	68,462	77,881
Reimbursable Expenses	1,393	10,416	(9,023)
Loan to Related Companies	214,925	45,000	169,925
Employee Advances	4,075		4,075
Prepaid Expenses	15,000	12,644	2,356
Undeposited Funds	1,094	-	1,094
Total Other Current Assets	236,487	68,060	168,428
Total Current Assets	**403,316**	**238,159**	**165,157**
Fixed Assets			
Leasehold Improvements	330,973	16,808	314,165
Vehicles	92,085	71,677	20,408
Computer Equipment	58,003	55,607	2,396
Office Furniture	89,682	60,651	29,030
Accumulated Depreciation	(163,896)	(158,021)	(5,875)
Total Fixed Assets	**406,847**	**46,722**	**360,124**

continued…

	Other Assets		
APS Deposit	3,867		3,867
Investments	118,000		118,000
Security Deposit: Lease	5,031	5,031	-
Total Other Assets	**126,898**	**5,031**	**121,867**
Total Assets	**937,061**	**289,912**	**647,149**

LIABILITIES

	Current Liabilities		
Accounts Payable	294,096	-	294,096
Total Accounts Payable	294,096	-	294,096
American Express Gold 2	-	255	(255)
Chase Ink Card 2	744	15,164	(14,420)
Total Chase Ink Card 2	744	15,419	(14,675)
Total Credit Cards	744	15,674	(14,930)
Arizona Department of Revenue Payable	750		750
Payroll Liabilities	13,531	901	12,630
Tenant Security Deposit	11,625		11,625
Wells Fargo Line of Credit	125,000		125,000
Current Portion of Long-Term Debt	12,000		
Total Other Current Liabilities	162,905	901	150,005
Total Current Liabilities	**457,745**	**16,575**	**429,170**
	Long-Term Liabilities		
US Bank Loan: Audi	54,220		54,220
Less Current Portion of Long-Term Debt	(12,000)		
Total Long-Term Liabilities	**42,220**	**-**	**42,220**
Total Liabilities	**499,965**	**16,575**	**471,390**

continued…

EQUITY			
Capital Stock	1,000	1,000	-
Retained Earnings	272,337	449,027	(176,690)
Shareholder Distributions	-	(166,850)	166,850
Taxes	-	(1,700)	1,700
Total Shareholder Distributions	-	(168,550)	168,550
Net Income	163,759	(8,141)	171,900
Total Equity	**437,096**	**273,337**	**163,759**
Total Liabilities & Equity	**937,061**	**289,912**	**647,149**

APPENDIX B:
Excellent Service Company Profit and Loss

	Jan–Dec 2017	Jan–Dec 2016	Change
Income			
CFO Services	1,082,145	279,475	802,670
Accounting Services	124,968	16,190	108,777
Retirement Plan Administration	12,181	3,939	8,242
Payroll Services	205,912	226,758	(20,846)
Tax Services	298,355	724,910	(426,555)
Consulting Services	102,808	175,896	(73,089)
Tax Controversy Services	24,130	8,360	15,770
Finance Charges	289	123	166
Discounts & Allowances	(1,790)	(106,804)	105,014
Total Income	**1,848,997**	**1,328,848**	**520,149**
Direct Client Costs			
Client Expenses	59,568	3,850	55,718
Client Service Guarantee	1,126	-	1,126
Total Direct Client Costs	**60,694**	**3,850**	**56,844**
Gross Profit	**1,788,303**	**1,324,998**	**463,305**
General & Admin Costs			
Auto Expense	13,127	8,452	4,675
Bad Debt Expense	-	46,783	(46,783)
Bank Charges & Merchant Fees	18,064	18,986	(922)
Charity	190		190
Dues & Subscriptions	7,256	3,735	3,522

continued…

Insurance	15,630	15,137	493
Interest Expense	2,253	912	1,342
Licenses & Permits	471	585	(114)
Miscellaneous	125	627	(502)
Office Expenses	17,263	26,994	(9,731)
Parking	218		218
Postage and Delivery	4,290	4,747	(457)
Professional Fees	14,649	3,512	11,137
Resource Materials	1,603	812	790
Telephone & Internet	20,829	22,753	(1,924)
Total General & Admin Costs	**115,969**	**154,036**	**(38,067)**

Occupancy Costs

Cleaning	2,427		2,427
Insurance	832	786	46
Landscaping/Plants	1,299	1,950	(651)
Moving & Storage	2,562		2,562
Property Taxes	12,597		12,597
Rent	112,670	55,444	57,226
Repairs & Maintenance	1,624	3,213	(1,589)
Television	467	701	(234)
Trash	201		201
Utilities	4,257		4,257
Total Occupancy Costs	**138,936**	**62,094**	**76,842**

Payroll

401(k) Match & Profit Sharing	25,735	31,177	(5,443)
Professionals	500,000	269,707	230,293

continued...

Administration	198,149	259,442	(61,294)
Bonus	51,803	24,453	27,350
Contract Services	9,900	31,659	(21,759)
Employee Expense Reimbursements	1,804	2,217	(413)
Health & Dental Insurance	52,583	54,105	(1,522)
Incentive Rewards	3,210	15,126	(11,916)
Life Insurance	2,701	860	1,841
Officer's Salary	75,772	85,682	(9,910)
Consulting Expense	180,006	43,000	137,006
Total Officer's Salary	255,778	128,682	127,096
Payroll Taxes	66,993	66,038	955
Professional Development	16,132	13,477	2,655
Recruiting	5,238	13,046	(7,808)
Staff Meals	9,612	7,769	1,843
Team Building	5,167	4,055	1,112
Workers' Comp	972	265	707
Total Payroll	**1,205,775**	**922,078**	**283,697**

Sales & Marketing

Advertising		563	(563)
Client Events	87	7,249	(7,162)
Client Rewards	332	5,771	(5,439)
Holiday	1,109	1,164	(55)
Marketing & Promotion	1,239	7,468	(6,229)
Meals & Entertainment	2,273	2,010	262
Networking	3,696	5,167	(1,470)
Printing and Reproduction	2,842	8,786	(5,944)

continued...

Public Relations	10,150		10,150
Referral Gifts	435	972	(537)
Sponsorship	3,959		3,959
Travel	10,281	6,996	3,285
Website	12,646	22,392	(9,746)
Total Sales & Marketing	**49,049**	**68,537**	**(19,488)**

Computer & Software Expenses

Computer Expenses	24,671	8,067	16,604
Software Expenses	80,441	84,687	(4,246)
Total Computer & Software Expenses	**105,112**	**92,754**	**12,358**
Total Expenses	**1,614,841**	**1,299,499**	**315,342**
Net Operating Income	**173,462**	**25,499**	**147,963**

Other Income

Gain/(Loss) on Fixed Assets	(20,439)	-	(20,439)
Interest Income	64	73	(9)
Other Income	34,875	58	34,817
Total Other Income	**14,500**	**131**	**14,369**

Other Expenses

Depreciation Expense	23,885	29,514	(5,629)
Life Insurance	318	4,257	(3,939)
Total Other Expenses	**24,203**	**33,771**	**(9,568)**
Net Other Income	**(9,703)**	**(33,640)**	**23,937**
Net Income	**163,759**	**(8,141)**	**171,900**

APPENDIX C:
Legal Cannabis Company Balance Sheet

	As of 12/31/17	As of 12/31/16	Change
ASSETS			
Current Assets			
ATM: Branch 1	13,681		13,681
ATM: Branch 2	12,280		12,280
ATM: Branch 3	6,700		6,700
Cash Account: Branch 1	37,266		37,266
Cash Account: Branch 2	24,789		24,789
Cash Account: Branch 3	27,506		27,506
Cash in Registers: Branch 1	1,000		1,000
Cash in Registers: Branch 2	1,000		1,000
Cash in Registers: Branch 3	700		700
Cash in Safe: Manufacturing Facility	835	495	340
Bank Trust Account	137,344	52,902	84,442
Operating Checking Account	22,781		22,781
Operating Payroll Account	58,021		58,021
Money Market Reserve Account	-	50,119	(50,119)
Total Bank Accounts	343,903	103,516	240,387
Total Accounts Receivable	18,000	-	18,000
Work in Process: Manufacturing Facility	90,379	104,610	(14,231)
Related Party Loan Receivable	27,674	-	27,674
3rd Party Inventory	76,538		76,538
Homegrown Inventory	19,061		19,061
Total Inventory: Branch 1	95,599	-	95,599

continued...

3rd Party Inventory	75,698		75,698
Homegrown Inventory	28,600		28,600
Total Inventory: Branch 2	104,298	-	104,298
3rd Party Inventory	72,843		72,843
Homegrown Inventory	106,336		106,336
Total Inventory: Branch 3	179,179	-	179,179
Inventory: Manufacturing Facility	624,771	476,084	148,687
Prepaid Expenses	185,724	62,657	123,067
Undeposited Funds	-	3,080	(3,080)
Total Other Current Assets	1,307,623	646,431	661,192
Total Current Assets	**1,669,527**	**749,947**	**919,580**
Fixed Assets			
Vehicles	44,960	13,068	31,892
Corporate Office Furniture	87,961	-	87,961
Corporate Office Equipment	3,122		3,122
Manufacturing Facility Machinery & Equipment	344,836	194,157	150,679
Manufacturing Facility: Security System	12,514		12,514
Store Fixtures & Equipment	199,610		199,610
Tenant Improvements	5,912,723	4,002,151	1,910,572
Accumulated Depreciation	(1,027,817)	(591,243)	(436,574)
Total Fixed Assets	**5,577,908**	**3,618,133**	**1,959,775**
Other Assets			
MMJ License: Branch 1	600,000		600,000
MMJ License: Branch 3	2,525,000		2,525,000
Security Deposit: Manufacturing Facility	114,000	114,000	0

continued…

Security Deposit: Corporate Office	4,214	-	4,214
Total Other Assets	**3,243,215**	**114,000**	**3,129,215**
Total Assets	**10,490,650**	**4,482,080**	**6,008,570**

LIABILITIES

Current Liabilities			
Total Accounts Payable	699,829	37,930	661,898
Bank CC 1234		21,171	(21,171)
Bank CC 5678	5,730	12,500	(6,770)
Total Credit Cards	5,730	33,671	(27,942)
Accrued Expenses	-	95,311	(95,311)
Accrued Interest	2,037	2,037	-
Accrued Personal Property Taxes	11,933	11,510	423
Accrued Property Taxes	26,738	7,406	19,332
Accrued Rent: Branch 2	126,000		126,000
Accrued Rent: Manufacturing Facility	1,837,905	1,555,904	282,001
Deferred Tax Liability	260,000	260,000	-
Payroll Liabilities	245,142	7,341	237,801
Sales Tax Payable: Branch 1	18,052		18,052
Sales Tax Payable: Branch 2	29,929		29,929
Sales Tax Payable: Branch 3	32,282		32,282
Current Portion of Long-Term Debt	1,200,000		1,200,000
Total Other Current Liabilities	**3,790,017**	**1,939,509**	**1,850,508**
Total Current Liabilities	**4,495,575**	**2,011,110**	**2,484,465**

continued...

	Long-Term Liabilities		
Shareholder Loans	8,041,874	2,737,921	5,303,953
Notes Payable: Honda Accord	27,496		27,496
Notes Payable: John Deere	17,467		17,467
Less Current Portion of Long-Term Debt	(1,200,000)		(1,200,000)
Total Long-Term Liabilities	**6,886,837**	**2,737,921**	**4,148,916**
Total Liabilities	**11,382,412**	**4,749,031**	**6,633,381**

EQUITY			
Retained Earnings	(266,951)	(945,181)	678,230
Net Income	(624,811)	678,230	(1,303,041)
Total Equity	**(891,762)**	**(266,951)**	**(624,811)**

Total Liabilities & Equity	**10,490,650**	**4,482,080**	**6,008,570**

APPENDIX D: Legal Cannabis Company Profit and Loss (January–December 2017)

	Corporate	Branch 1	Branch 2	Branch 3	TOTAL
		Income			
Consulting Income	600,000				600,000
Sales		2,900,477	3,752,621	716,982	7,370,080
Cash Over/(Short)		26,462	(4,133)	241	22,570
Gratuities			110		110
Refunds		(180)	(25)		(205)
Total Income	**600,000**	**2,926,759**	**3,748,573**	**717,223**	**7,992,555**
		Cost of Goods Sold			
Medical Director		9,000	11,000	3,000	23,000
Security Guards/Alarm	13,100	136,615	341,828	63,177	554,719
Total Applied Overhead	13,100	145,615	352,828	66,177	577,719
Cost of Goods Sold		1,720,669	1,927,291	650,299	4,298,259
Supplies				1,320	1,320
Total Direct Costs		1,720,669	1,927,291	651,619	4,299,579
Total Cost of Goods Sold	**13,100**	**1,866,283**	**2,280,119**	**717,796**	**4,877,298**
Gross Profit	**586,900**	**1,060,476**	**1,468,454**	**(573)**	**3,115,257**

continued....

General & Administrative Costs

Accounting	135,959		23,336		159,358
Automobile Expense	8,232	63	110	174	8,708
Banking & Cash Security	10,541	192	12,738	8	21,670
Computer and Internet Expenses	33,365	(1,616)	38,370	10,541	99,509
Consultants	343,183	17,233	-		343,183
Contracted Management	78,868		-		78,868
Dues and Subscriptions	736	4,375	4,581	4,375	14,067
Insurance Expense	68,859	32,334	76,105	19,635	196,933
Interest Expense	1,549		-		1,549
Legal & Professional Fees	97,250	27,795	19,765	4,385	149,195
Licenses & Permits	13,268	12,656	14,982	325	41,231
Miscellaneous Expense	2,152		4,600		6,752
Office Supplies	23,118	9,145	24,475	6,344	63,082
Postage and Delivery	356	353	210		919
Printing and Reproduction	10,984	581	19,989	126	31,680
Royalties			-	49,000	49,000
Software & Licensing	57,432	5,238	3,848	1,550	68,068
Total General & Administrative	**885,851**	**108,348**	**243,109**	**96,465**	**1,333,773**

continued...

Marketing & Promotion Costs

Advertising	357,262	71,252	105,931	18,020	552,465
Clothing	6,537				6,537
Market Research	628	74	1,820		2,522
Meals & Entertainment	1,866	119	139	15	2,139
Travel Expense	9,814	8	1,350	10	11,182
Web Design	20,051				20,051
Total Marketing & Promotion	**396,158**	**71,453**	**109,240**	**18,045**	**594,896**

Occupancy Costs

Alarm Monitoring: Stores	3,931	2,903	3,905	3,321	14,060
Property Taxes		6,251	29,426	2,970	38,647
Remodeling Expense		2,665			2,665
Rent Expense	61,013		126,000		187,013
Repairs and Maintenance	269	5,433	13,509	4,114	23,325
Telephone Expense	3,869	1,227	1,131	3,591	9,818
Utilities	479	11,672	30,253	6,646	49,049
Total Occupancy Costs	**69,561**	**30,151**	**204,223**	**20,641**	**324,577**

continued...

	Staffing Costs			
Continuing Education	2,167			2,167
Employee Expense Reimbursements	5,318	(282)		5,036
Employee Incentives	52,414	1,020	2,963	56,397
Health Insurance	87,917	(3,681)	(7,139)	(2,734)	74,363
Management Salaries	446,741		-	446,741
Outside Labor	720	3,170	-	3,890
Payroll Processing Fees	4,363	95	-	75	4,533
Payroll Taxes	37,309	24,492	42,492	8,567	112,860
Recruiting	3,374		-	3,374
Salaries & Wages	13,983	257,644	436,056	94,603	802,287
Staff Meals	2,159	1,553	1,277	253	5,242
Uniforms	2,010		-	2,010
Total Staffing Costs	**658,476**	**284,011**	**475,649**	**100,765**	**1,518,901**
Total Expenses	**2,010,045**	**493,964**	**1,002,796**	**235,916**	**3,742,720**
Net Operating Income	**(1,423,145)**	**566,512**	**465,658**	**(236,489)**	**(627,464)**

continued...

374 · PROTECT YOUR PROFIT

Other Income

ATM Fees		58		58
TPT Accounting Credit	1,429	1,913	284	3,627
Total Other Income	**1,429**	**1,971**	**284**	**3,684**

Other Expenses

Charitable Contributions	342	-		342
Corporate Tax	100	-		100
Penalties & Fees	108	384	98	590
Total Other Expenses	**550**	**384**	**98**	**1,032**
Net Other Income	**(550)**	**1,045**	**1,873**	**284**	**2,652**
Net Income	**(1,423,695)**	**567,558**	**467,531**	**(236,205)**	**(624,811)**

APPENDIX · 375